Leav
Phi

T0228562

methuen | drama
LONDON • NEW YORK • OXFORD • NEW DELHI • SYDNEY

METHUEN DRAMA
Bloomsbury Publishing Plc
50 Bedford Square, London, WC1B 3DP, UK
1385 Broadway, New York, NY 10018, USA
29 Earlsfort Terrace, Dublin 2, Ireland

BLOOMSBURY, METHUEN DRAMA and the Methuen
Drama logo are trademarks of Bloomsbury Publishing Plc

First published in Great Britain 2007

This edition published 2023

Cover artwork by Mark Senior

A catalogue record for this book is available from the British Library.

A catalog record for this book is available from the Library of Congress.

ISBN: PB: 978-1-3504-2182-0
ePDF: 978-1-3504-2184-4
eBook: 978-1-3504-2183-7

Series: Modern Plays

Typeset by Mark Heslington Ltd, Scarborough, North Yorkshire

To find out more about our authors and books visit
www.bloomsbury.com and sign up for our newsletters.

Leaves of Glass

Written by **Philip Ridley**

Directed by **Max Harrison**

Produced by **Lidless Theatre** and **Zoe Weldon**, in
association with **Theatre Deli** and **Park Theatre**.

About Park Theatre

Park Theatre was founded by Artistic Director Jez Bond and Creative Director Emeritus Melli Marie. The building opened in May 2013 and, with eight West End transfers, two National Theatre transfers and 13 national tours in its first ten years, quickly garnered a reputation as a key player in the London theatrical scene. Park Theatre has received six Olivier nominations, won numerous Off West End Offie Awards, and won *The Stage*'s Fringe Theatre of the Year and Accessible Theatre Award.

Park Theatre is an inviting and accessible venue, delivering work of exceptional calibre in the heart of Finsbury Park. We work with writers, directors and designers of the highest quality to present compelling, exciting and beautifully told stories across our two intimate spaces.

Our programme encompasses a broad range of work from classics to revivals with a healthy dose of new writing, producing in-house as well as working in partnership with emerging and established producers. We strive to play our part within the UK's theatre ecology by offering mentoring, support and opportunities to artists and producers within a professional theatre-making environment.

Our Creative Learning strategy seeks to widen the number and range of people who participate in theatre, and provides opportunities for those with little or no prior contact with the arts.

In everything we do we aim to be warm and inclusive; a safe, welcoming and wonderful space in which to work, create and visit.

★ ★ ★ ★ ★
'A five-star neighbourhood theatre.'
Independent

As a registered charity [number 1137223] with no public subsidy, we rely on the kind support of our donors and volunteers. To find out how you can get involved visit **parktheatre.co.uk**

Cast

Liz
Kacey Ainsworth

Debbie
Katie Buchholz

Steven
Ned Costello

Barry
Joseph Potter

Creatives

Writer
Philip Ridley

Director
Max Harrison

Set & Costume Designer
Kit Hinchcliffe

Lighting Designer
Alex Lewer

Sound Designer
Sam Glossop

Assistant Director
Katarina Fuller

Casting Consultant
Nadine Rennie CDG

Fight & Intimacy Director
Lawrence Carmichael

Movement Consultant
Sam Angell

Accent Coach
Mary Howland

Stage Manager
Brains

PR
Kevin Wilson PR

Marketing
Cup of Ambition

Poster Image
Mark Senior

Graphic Designer
Marshall Stay

Thanks to:

Theatre Deli, East15, Peter Dicks, Ray Cooney, Jennifer Greenbury, Bobby Allen, Michael Hacking, Stage One, Feargus Woods Dunlop and Sofi Berenger

Leaves of Glass was first presented by Soho Theatre, London, directed by Lisa Goldman, on 3 May 2007.

By arrangement with Knight Hall Agency Ltd.

Kacey Ainsworth
Liz

Theatre Credits Include: *LAVA* (Soho Theatre & UK Tour); *Sweeney Todd* (Liverpool Everyman); *Holes* (Nottingham Playhouse); *Feed the Beast* (Birmingham Rep/New Wolsey Theatre, Stephen Joseph Theatre); *Calendar Girls* (National Theatre Tour); *Steel Magnolias* (ATG); *Carrie's War* (Apollo West End); *Attempts on Her Life* (Royal Court); *Sleep With Me* (Royal National Theatre); *Serving It Up* (Bush Theatre); and *Pale Horse* (Royal Court Upstairs).

Television Credits Include: *Grantchester* (ITV); *Sliced* (Dave); *Moving On* (BBC); *The Worst Witch* (Netflix); *Call the Midwife* (BBC); *Casualty* (BBC); *The Wright Way* (BBC); *Midsomer Murders* (Bentley Productions); *The Moonstone* (BBC); *Rock Chips* (BBC); *Holby Blue* (BBC); *Hotel Babylon* (BBC); *Eastenders* (BBC); *The Beggar Bride* (BBC); *The Accused* (BBC).

Film Credits Include: *Lynne and Lucy* (BBC); *Mother* (Townley Productions); *We The Kings* (Elemo Films); *Hip Hip Hooray* (Lyndsey Miller); *Girl From Rio* (Casanova Pictures); *Topsy Turvey* (Thin Man Films). Kacey won most popular actress at the National Television Awards in 2002.

Radio Credits Include: *Torchwood* (Big Finish); *Dr Who* (Big Finish).

Katie Buchholz
Debbie

Theatre Credits Include: Bernadette Understudy in *Lemons Lemons Lemons Lemons Lemons* (Harold Pinter Theatre); Nina/Masha Understudy in *The Seagull* (Jamie Lloyd Company); *Eigengrau* (Waterloo East); *Mary Stuart* (Almeida); *Peregrine* (Stockwell Playhouse); *If We Were Older* (National); *Women on the Edge* (John Thaw Studio); *A Little Night Music* (Garrick); *Inherit the Wind* (Old Vic); *Mary Poppins* (Prince Edward).

TV Credits Include: *Deceit* (Channel 4); *Eastenders* (BBC); *Father Brown* (BBC).

Ned Costello
Steven

Theatre Credits Include: *The Clothes They Stood Up in* (Nottingham Playhouse, Directed by Adam Penford); *Britannicus* (Lyric Hammersmith, Directed by Atri Banerjee).

TV Credits Include: *Wreck* (BBC); *The Capture* Series 2 (BBC).

Joseph Potter
Barry

Theatre Credits Include: *Salt Water Moon* (Finborough); *The Poltergeist* (Arcola Theatre & Southwark Playhouse – OFFIE Award Winner for Best Actor); *The Dwarfs* (White Bear); *Candida* (Orange Tree); *The Beast of Blue Yonder* (Southwark Playhouse); *Mercury Fur, Fury, Orestes, Romeo & Juliet* (Guildhall).

TV Credits Include: *Father Brown, Casualty* (BBC); *All At Sea* (CBBC).

Film Credits Include: *My Policeman*.

Philip Ridley

Writer

Philip was born and grew up in the East End of London. He studied painting at St Martin's School of Art. He has written many highly regarded and hugely influential stage plays: the seminal *The Pitchfork Disney* (now published as a Methuen Modern Classic); *The Fastest Clock in the Universe* (winner of a Time Out Award, the Critics' Circle Award for Most Promising Playwright, and the Meyer-Whitworth Prize); *Ghost from a Perfect Place*; *Vincent River* (nominated for the London Festival Fringe Best Play Award); the highly controversial *Mercury Fur*; *Leaves of Glass*; *Piranha Heights* (nominated for the WhatsOnStage Mobius Award for Best Off West End Production); *Tender Napalm* (nominated for the London Fringe Best Play Award); *Shivered* (nominated for the OffWestEnd Best New Play Award); *Dark Vanilla Jungle* (winner of an Edinburgh Festival Fringe First Award); *Radiant Vermin* (now published as a Methuen Modern Classic); *Tonight With Donny Stixx*; *Karagula* (nominated for the OffWestEnd Best New Play Award); *The Beast of Blue Yonder*; *The Poltergeist* (winner of the OffWestEnd OnComm Award for Best Live Streamed Play); and *Tarantula*; plus several plays for young people (collectively known as *The Storyteller Sequence*): *Karamazoo*, *Fairytaleheart*, *Moonfleece* (named as one of the 50 Best Works About Cultural Diversity by the National Centre for Children's Books), the seminal *Sparkleshark* (the first of the Connections Festival plays for young people to be staged professionally by the National Theatre); *Brokenville* and *Feathers in the Snow* (shortlisted for the Brian Way Best Play Award).

Max Harrison

Director

After training at LAMDA as an actor, Max set up his own theatre company, Lidless Theatre, and has since directed at leading London fringe venues including The Pleasance, Southwark Playhouse and The King's Head Theatre. He studied under the tutelage of Mike Alfred (Shared Experience, National Theatre) and went on to Assist him on *Five Characters in Search of a Good Night's Sleep* (Southwark Playhouse). He is excited to be working with Philip Ridley for a third time, after a five-star production of *Moonfleece* and *Tender Napalm*.

Kit Hinchcliffe

Set & Costume Designer

Kit trained at Central St Martins College of Art and Design. Since graduating, her work has spanned theatre, dance and installation. She is Co-Artistic Director of Lidless Theatre and regularly collaborates with Architecture Social Club as Designer/Fabricator.

Work includes: *Oresteia* (Corbett Theatre); *The Journey to Venice* (Finborough Theatre); *Camino Real* and *Cymbeline* (Bridewell Theatre); *Mapping Gender* (BALTIC Centre for Contemporary Art, Cambridge Junction and The Place); *A Hideous*

Monstrous Verminous Creature (The Place); *La bohème* (King's Head Theatre); *Boys* (Barbican Centre); *Festen* (Corbett Theatre); *Tender Napalm* (King's Head Theatre); *Well Lit* (Dansstationen Malmö and The Place); *Moonfleece* (Pleasance); *Pebbles* (Katzpace); *Heroes* (Bridge House Theatre); *Beetles from the West* (Hope Theatre); *Fundamentals* (Platform TheatreKX).

Alex Lewer
Lighting Designer

Recent work includes: *F**cking Men* (Waterloo East); *Vermin* (Arcola Theatre); *Bright Half Life* (Kings Head Theatre); *Clybourne Park* (Park Theatre); *Love Story – The 10th Anniversary in Concert* (Cadogan Hall); *Lipstick* (Southwark Playhouse); *The Green Fairy* and *Striking 12* (The Union Theatre); Simon Stephens' *One Minute* (Vaults Theatre, Off West End Award Nominee for Best Lighting Design). *Alexlewer.com*

Sam Glossop
Sound Designer

Sam is a Sound Designer and Composer from Sheffield.

Recent work includes: *Rock/Paper/Scissors* (Lyceum, Sheffield Theatres); *Home* (Minerva, Chichester Festival Theatre); *Much Ado About Nothing* (Crucible, Ramps On The Moon & Sheffield Theatres); *Flinch* (UK Tour); *Around the World In Eighty Days* (The Barn Theatre); *Leaves of Glass* (The Park Theatre); *The Legend of Sleepy Hollow* (UK Tour); *Peter Pan* (Reading Rep); *Doctor Faustus, Instructions for a*

Teenage Armageddon (Southwark Playhouse); *Gracie* (Finborough Theatre); *Dead Good* (UK Tour); *The Tempest* and *A Midsummer Night's Dream* (Greenwich Theatre); *Where is Peter Rabbit?* (Theatre Royal Haymarket / Hong Kong and Singapore tour).

Zoe Weldon
Producer

Zoe is a Stage One Bursary recipient. She is a Freelance Producer as well as an Associate Producer at the King's Head Theatre. Zoe has previously worked in the West End for Sonia Friedman Productions, Bill Kenwright Productions and ATG. Freelance work includes: *Instructions for a Teenage Armageddon* (Southwark Playhouse, Offie Finalist); *Tender Napalm* (King's Head Theatre; Offie-nominated); *Brawn* (King's Head Theatre); *Jew...ish* (King's Head Theatre, Edinburgh Fringe Festival and Drayton Arms; Offie-nominated); *CHUTNEY* (Bunker Theatre; Offie-nominated); *Snapshot* (Hope Theatre); *Quandary* (Reading, RADA); *Mind The Gap* (Edinburgh Fringe Festival). Zoe has also worked with Rifco Theatre producing their 21 Years Celebratory event and with Debbie Hicks Productions as an Assistant Producer on *Ages of the Moon* and *The Permanent Way* (Vaults Theatre).

Lidless Theatre

Lidless Theatre is an established London based theatre company that focuses on making raw and emotionally impactful theatre through human stories. Some of our plays have political dimensions, some have social dimensions, others tackle human rights, but we believe above all the **shared human experience** is the most **vital** and **intrinsic** aspect of the theatre and so we centre our work around that.

www.lidlesstheatre.com

We are made up of a director, a producer, and a designer. We have an established relationship with Philip Ridley, having staged three revivals of his work. We are working closely with emerging playwrights to develop new work.

Lidless Theatre is also dedicated to developing acting talent and run regular Meisner workshops.

Theatre Deli

Theatre Deli occupies unused spaces in city centres and transforms them into creative communities. The charity provides space, support and resources to artists at all stages of their careers in order to develop and share new art and performance. It also presents a wide programme of events and shows, and hosts hundreds of classes and workshops every year. Founded in 2007, the organisation has occupied 12 meanwhile venues in Sheffield and London, and opened its first long-term venue in Sheffield in 2023. Its current London space is located on Leadenhall Street in the City of London.

www.theatredeli.co.uk

Foreword

Leaves of Glass by Philip Ridley has always been one of my favourite plays. I love its subtlety, its beauty, and its accumulative – breathtaking – sucker punch. I've wanted to work on it in it for years. And now – right now – it feels more relevant than ever.

The play is about memory. How we use – manipulate – a particular narrative of the past to shape the story of our lives. Currently, we seem to be surrounded by people apparently doing exactly that. Think Amber Heard and Johnny Depp. Think Prince William and Prince Harry. All with totally differing interpretations of what has happened. All totally convinced 'their truth' is the only truth. And all totally willing to go down in flames to prove it.

Leaves of Glass looks at how elusive memory can be. The lies we tell ourselves (and others). And the power that's eventually held by the person who seizes controls of the narrative. Nowhere is that battle for narrative more vivid, more complex and more potentially explosive than in a family. What Ridley has done with this play is take the story of an everyday East London family, and invest it with all the tension, suspense and intrigue of a political thriller.

At the bottom line, what I'm really interested in is a gripping story, a theatrical experience, and an emotional journey. Ridley's plays always have these things. In abundance. But *Leaves of Glass*, for me, builds to a tidal wave of feeling that puts it in a league of its own.

Max Harrison

Leaves of Glass

For Charlotte Knight

*We are the veil that veils us
from ourselves.*
R. D. Laing

*Commit a crime, and the earth
is made of glass.*
Wallace Stevens

My secrets cry aloud.
Theodore Roethke

Characters

Steven
Barry
Debbie
Liz

1

Steven, *twenty-seven*.

Steven I remember . . . one Sunday morning Dad said,
'Get in the car, boys.' Barry asked, 'Where we going, Dad?'
'A surprise.' I sit in the front because I'm the oldest. Fifteen.
Barry's in the back getting all excited and jabbering away.
He acts a bit young for his age sometimes. He's ten.

Beat.

Dad parks the car and says, 'Everybody out!' Seagulls! Barry
asks if we're near the seaside. Dad laughs and takes Barry's
hand. He goes to take mine but I pull it away. I'm not a kid.
We walk down a street. Barry is doing that half-skipping
thing and tugging Dad's arm. I tell Barry to calm down. It's
one thing to be happy but you don't have to broadcast it to
the whole bloody world, do you . . . Well, *do* you?

Beat.

Barry says, 'Look! The Thames!' And there it is. We're right
by the river. And then I see – Silver! Big silver things across
the water. I know what it is. Dad was talking about it last
week. The Thames Barrier. Dad explained how if the river
gets too high the Barrier would lift up these . . . these – like
big doors or something. And it would hold all the water
back. Barry said, 'I'd like to see the Thames Barrier, Dad.'
And – hey presto! – here we are. Dad usually gives Barry
what he wants. Barry's his favourite. I don't mind. I'm
Mum's favourite so it sort of balances out. Well, *don't* it?

Beat.

Barry says the Barrier looks like a row of silver pyramids. I
tell him not really because a pyramid has to be pyramid
shaped. And those silver things are shaped like . . . well, not
pyramids. Barry says he's gonna do a drawing of it for Dad
when he gets home. Dad says he'd love a drawing of silver
pyramids. Barry's good at drawing.

Beat.

And then . . . then this gust of wind comes along – real strong – and . . . and Dad – he grabs hold of my hand. So sudden. So tight. His nails dig in. I try to pull away but Dad just holds tighter and tighter. I look at him. The scar by his left eye is sort of twitching. Like it does when Mum's shouting at him and he don't say a single word back. I say, 'Dad . . . you're hurting me!' But still he won't let go. I can see he's holding Barry's hand just as hard. Barry's face is all screwed up. Again I say, 'Dad! You're *still* hurting me.' Again his grip gets tighter. It's as if . . . as if Dad's afraid the gust of wind is going to blow me and Barry away . . . and he'll lose us forever.

2

Barry's *flat.*

Barry, *twenty-two, is on floor.*

Steven *is standing.*

Barry   Not going there.

Steven   Barry?

Barry   Don't make me . . . don't . . .

Steven's *phone rings.*

Answers it.

Steven   Hi, Jan . . . At Barry's . . . Yeah, yeah, he's here but – Eh? . . . Well, it's what we expected. Had to break the door open again. Well, the people downstairs did.

Barry   I don't want to!

Steven   Hear him? – Eh? . . . I *have* tried – Barry? . . . *Barry*?! – Jesus! There's a bucket full of vomit . . . Eh? . . . Oh, it's not just the *drink* doing it . . . Don't know. Don't *want* to know.

Barry   He'll hurt me!

Steven   No one's going to hurt you! (*Into phone.*) Eh? . . .
No, no, I'll stay till he surfaces. Cancel everything for the
rest of the day . . . He's my brother, Jan, what else can I do?

Barry *cries out.*

Steven   Oh, and Jan. Not a word in the office. If anyone
asks tell them . . . tell them me and Barry are doing
something for our mum –

Barry *wakes with a gasp.*

Steven   It's all right, brov.

Barry   Steve!

Steven (*into phone*)   Well, at least he knows me.

Barry   Who're you talking to?

Grabs **Steven***'s phone and* –

Barry (*into phone*)   Leave me alone!

Steven   Stop it, Barry.

Grabs phone back and –

(*Into phone.*) Janis? I'll phone you back.

Hangs up.

Pull yourself together!

Barry   If we stick together we'll be all right.

Steven   I'll make some coffee.

Barry   We can get weapons! Baseball bats with . . . with
nails sticking out like . . . like medieval things.

Steven   Jesus, Barry, where *is* everything? No coffee.
No tea.

Barry   Bash! His brains will spill out.

Steven   The milk's off!

Barry   I'll chop him up.

Steven   Chop *who* up?

Barry   Him! *Him!* I'll put his pieces into this bucket – Don't look, brov! It'll make you feel sick. I'll cover it up.

Uses his T-shirt.

That better?

Steven   Yes. Thank you.

Barry   A funeral, brov! We should have a funeral! We'll send out invites! Where shall we ask people to come? . . . Mum's garden! We'll bury him there! I'll dig lots of holes and – Throw the bits in. Dig! Throw! Dig! Throw! Dig! Throw! Dig! – Steve! Look!

Steven   What?

Barry   The bits of him are growing! Growing like trees! I'll chop them down, brov! Chop! Chop! Chop! It's no good! They're growing too fast! Help me, brov! Chop! Chop! Why won't you help me?

Steven   Barry –

Barry   We're in a forest! We might get lost! Is that what you want, brov? Lost in a forest of . . . of *him*?

Steven   Who *is* this 'him'?

Barry   You know who.

Steven   No, I don't.

Barry   You do.

Steven   I don't.

Barry   . . . You *do*.

Steven   . . . I *don't*.

3

Steven's *house.*

Steven *is looking out of window.*

Debbie, *thirty-two, enters with shopping.*

Debbie   Oh! You scared me.

Steven   Sorry.

Debbie   Thought you were at the office.

Steven   I was.

Debbie   I've walked miles.

Steven   I've been ringing you.

Debbie   Oh?

Checks phone.

Dead. Sorry. Anything wrong?

Steven   No, no. I just wanted to . . .

Debbie   To?

Steven   . . . Say hello.

Debbie   . . . Hello.

Steven   Hello.

They embrace.

Debbie   Steve . . .

Steven   I rang Barry.

Debbie   How was he?

Steven   Fine. Sounded like he was out having fun somewhere.

Debbie   You won't catch *him* working on a Saturday.

Steven   *I'm* not working on a Saturday. I'm here.

Debbie   What're you *doing* here?

Steven   I . . . I'm looking out the window.

Debbie   At what? Cement mixers. Scaffolding.

Steven   Oh, it's not that bad.

Debbie   It's worse.

Steven   Not if you're careful how you look.

Debbie   Careful how I –?

Steven   Squint a bit. Go on.

Debbie   Steve . . .

Steven   Come on, Deb. Let it blur.

Debbie *squints.*

Steven   What d'you see?

Debbie   I see . . .

Steven   Mmm?

Debbie   No more cement mixers.

Steven   That's it! No more scaffolding.

Debbie   Workmen – all gone.

Steven   Everything finished.

Debbie   Perfect houses.

Steven   That shadow –

Debbie   I'm pregnant.

Beat.

Steven   When?

Debbie   *Now.* I'm pregnant *now.*

Steven   But . . .

Debbie We can start decorating that spare room. Like we said.

Steven *What* did we say?

Debbie Nursery.

Steven We *said* that?

Debbie I've seen the perfect cot.

Steven Debbie? You're *sure*?

Debbie Sure?

Steven Baby.

Debbie Confirmed this afternoon.

Steven 'Confirmed'?

Debbie At the hospital.

Steven I thought . . .

Debbie What?

Steven Your sister? Shopping?

Debbie I was. We were.

Indicates shopping.

Steven So you . . .

Debbie Hospital. *Then* shopping.

Steven With Cleo?

Debbie With Cleo – New handbag!

Steven But –

Debbie You said it's what you *wanted*, Steve.

Steven What I –?

Debbie A baby!

Steven Oh! Well, it's . . . *Did* I say –?

Debbie   Tick tock!

Steven   What?

Debbie   Body clock.

Steven   Oh. Yes.

Debbie   It's what we need.

Steven   *Need?*

Debbie   For *us*. You know?

Steven   I –

Debbie   *Please*, Steve. Let's just . . . We'll be happy.

Steven *doesn't react.*

Beat.

Debbie   Cleo *said* you'd be like this!

Steven   Like what?

Debbie   *This!* . . . We were walking out of the hospital and I said, 'Steve's going to be *so* happy,' and she went, 'Mmm' in that way she does –

Steven   She's never liked me.

Debbie   Not true! I said, 'What's *that* supposed to mean, Cleo?' and she said, 'He'll just give you that look of his.'

Steven   *What* 'look'?

Debbie   I said, 'Of course he won't, Cleo,' and she said, 'He will, Debs,' and now I've told you and . . . You *are*! – What's it called again?

Steven   It's got a *name*?

Debbie   Something to do with war.

Steven   War? You've been talking to Barry.

Debbie   No. Cleo.

Steven   What's Cleo know about war?

Debbie   When she was in that play. Remember?

Steven   No.

Debbie   The raped girl thing.

Steven   What raped girl –?

Debbie   Soldiers burst into that girl's house. Raped her. Shot her. And the girl's parents. Then set fire to the whole caboodle and went back to base camp calm as cucumbers.

Steven   That.

Debbie   What people are capable of, eh? Awful. Makes you think . . . I need a bath!

Steven   The 'look', Debbie.

Debbie   Eh?

Steven   This look I'm supposed to –

Debbie   Oh! Soldiers get it. They just stare – 'Thousand yard stare'! *That's* it! That's *you!*

Steven   I don't know why you keep –

Debbie   I rush home from the hospital. Best news ever. Other men'd jump for joy and . . . whatever. You? Oh, no! But a kiss. A simple little kiss. Is that too much to . . .? Jesus!

Slight pause.

Steven *kisses* **Debbie.**

4

Liz's *house.*

Steven *and* **Debbie** *are seated.*

Liz, *fifty-two, enters with tray.*

Liz   My grandmother used to tell me –

Steven   Careful, Mum.

Liz   I can manage – (*At* **Debbie**.) He thinks I'm a whatsit.

Debbie   Damsel in distress.

Steven   I don't think / you're a damsel in –

Liz   I've buried two parents and a husband, I think I'm capable of carrying some tea and biscuits.

Steven   Debbie don't take sugar anymore, Mum.

Liz   I know, I know.

Debbie   I can speak for myself.

Liz   One without the spoon, love.

Debbie *takes cup and saucer.*

Liz   Biscuits?

Debbie   No thanks, Liz.

Liz   What was I saying?

Steven   Grandmother.

Liz   Teeth!

Steven   Teeth?

Liz   Women used to have a few out. Every time.

Steven   Every time *what*?

Liz   They got pregnant.

Steven   No.

Liz   He thinks I'm stupid.

Steven   I *don't* think / you're stupid.

Debbie   I've *heard* about this. My sister told me.

Liz (*at* **Steven**)   You see?

Steven   Well, *I've* never heard of –

Liz   Take it, then, take it.

Offering tray to **Steven**.

Steven   What one?

Liz   *That* one.

Steven *takes a cup of tea*.

Liz   Not too much milk in it, is there?

Steven   No, it's fine.

Liz   I can make you another – (*At* **Debbie**.) He's so fussy.

Debbie   Oh, I know.

Steven   I am *not* fussy.

Liz   Biscuit?

Steven   No, thanks.

Liz   I've brought them in now.

Steven *takes a biscuit*.

Debbie   Calcium.

Liz   That's right!

Steven   What?

Debbie   Woman's teeth used it all up.

Liz   Calcium.

Debbie   Baby's bones wouldn't grow.

Liz   They used to pull the mum's teeth out.

Debbie   So their calcium went to the baby.

Steven   Well, *I've* never heard / of anything like –

Debbie   It *happened*, Steve!

Beat.

Then –

Liz   I've seen the perfect little cot for the baby.

Steven   Really?

Liz   Cherubs all over.

Steven   Sounds great, Mum.

Debbie   We've already *got* a cot, Liz.

Steven   It hasn't been delivered yet.

Debbie   It *will* be.

Steven   We can cancel.

Debbie   I don't *want* to cancel.

Beat.

Then –

Liz   Your brother told me how thrilled he was about being an uncle. Thrilled! He says he's gonna do a painting of the baby soon as it's born.

Debbie *sips tea and winces.*

Debbie   Ugh! Liz.

Liz   Sugar?

Debbie *nods.*

Liz   Sorry, love – Try yours, Steve.

Steven *sips tea.*

Steven   Sugar.

Liz (*at* **Debbie**)   You must've taken mine.

Debbie *swaps her tea with* **Liz***'s.*

Liz Gran saw this pregnant woman held down once. Her husband grabbed some pliers and yanked out *all* her teeth. The screams! The blood!

Steven Mum!

Liz What?

Indicates **Debbie**.

Debbie I'm pregnant, not ill.

Liz He thinks you're a shrinking violet.

Steven I do *not* think / she's a shrinking violet.

Debbie It's *him* who's the shrinking violet.

Liz He is.

Steven I'm *not*.

Debbie You're squeamish.

Steven 'Squeamish'?!

Liz You are.

Steven I don't know why you both / keep picking on me?

Debbie He can't look at *any* of the books I've bought.

Steven I *do* look at / the books you've –

Debbie Not the pictures of a birth you don't.

Liz He's just like his dad.

Steven I am *not* like Dad!

Liz Passed out in the delivery room. / Flat on his face. Nearly lost an eye.

Steven You can't . . . you can't just . . . blurt something out / like that out and –

Liz 'Blurt'? Who's blurting?

Debbie (*at* **Steven**)   What's bloody got into you?

Liz   He needs a holiday.

Steven   I do *not* need / a bloody holiday.

Debbie   He *hates* holidays.

Liz   He can't relax.

Steven   I *can*.

Debbie   You're not *now*.

Liz   He works too hard.

Debbie   You're stressed.

Liz   Your dad used to get stressed.

Steven   Jesus!

Liz   Frank was too sensitive. He was the first man I ever saw cry. It'll be twelve years since he died in October. You know that, Steve?

Steven   Yes, I know that, Mum.

Liz   He would've *loved* a grandchild, wouldn't he?

Steven *doesn't respond.*

Liz   *Steven!?*

Dog barks next door.

Oh, no, not again.

Steven   I'll go next door and complain if you like.

Liz   It gets *worse* if you complain.

Debbie   You need double glazing.

Steven   That's what *I* said.

Liz   *You* promised to get me some.

Steven   *You* said you didn't want all the mess.

Liz   I *don't* want all the mess – (*At* **Debbie**.) Who wants mess?

Debbie   It'll be worth it to keep the noise out, Liz.

Steven (*at* **Liz**)   Exactly!

Liz   It's coming through the walls, not the windows.

Steven   *Now* it is, but not *all* the time.

Liz   *Most* of the time.

Steven   *Some* of the time.

Liz   I'm not destroying my home for –

Steven   'Destroying'?!

Liz   Oh, listen to it! Shut up! *Shut up!*

Steven   I'll write to the landlords.

Liz   It's the landlords who're behind it.

Steven   No.

Liz   It's a plot.

Steven   'A plot'?!

Liz   Conspiracy! They want to drive me out.

Debbie   They want to turn your house into flats, Liz.

Liz   They do.

Debbie   More money.

Liz   Greed.

Debbie   Money.

Liz   Pure greed.

Debbie *sips tea.*

Debbie   Ugh! Liz.

Liz   Oh, no. Not sugar in *all* of them? It's that bloody dog! Confusing me. Bark, bark, bark!

Steven   Here, give me the tray.

Liz   I'm all right.

Steven   But you're going to drop it –

Liz   DON'T TOUCH ME! *DON'T!*

5

Steve's *office*.

Steve *and* **Barry**.

Barry   I owe you an explanation.

Steven   Forget it, Barry.

Barry   I can't. We're brothers. You trusted me and I let you down.

Steven   No.

Barry   Please, Steve. I can't rest until I . . . *Please.*

Beat.

It was really shitty weather this morning. Early. You see it?

Steven   Yeah.

Barry   Grey sky. Grey people. All colour sucked out. You know those old photos from the First World War?

Steven   What?

Barry   The trenches.

Steven   Those.

Barry   That's what it felt like. Shot at dawn weather. That's what they should call a mornings like that. On weather forecasts. You know? 'It's gonna be shot at dawn weather.' Then we'd all know what they mean. Well, *I* would. Wouldn't you, Steve?

Steven   Well, I will now.

Barry They shot boys. Shell-shocked boys.

Steven Terrible.

Barry The boys were crying but the men still – Ready! Aim! . . . What was I saying?

Steven Miserable morning.

Barry Bloody miserable. And I was standing on that corner where I always stand. Waiting for Jacko and Marky-boy. And they were a bit late and –

Steven So *that's* it!

Barry What?

Steven Why didn't you *tell* me they were late?

Barry It was nothing. A few minutes.

Steven *I* would've been in a bad mood / too if I'd been kept –

Barry Jacko and Marky-boy being late had nothing to do with . . . what happened later. Okay?

Beat.

I see the truck coming down the road and Jacko gives his usual three beeps and I squeeze in next to Marky-boy and we drive off and I look at Jacko and Marky-boy and . . . and . . .

Beat.

Steven *What*, brov?

Barry You'll think I'd been drinking.

Steven I won't.

Barry I've stopped. *All* of it.

Steven I know.

Barry No drink. Nothing.

Steven   I know.

Barry   You know that, don't you.

Steven   . . . Yes . . . I know.

Beat.

Barry   Guess what they looked like.

Steven   Who?

Barry   Jacko and Marky-boy.

Steven   I . . . I'm not / sure what you –

Barry   You know those photos from Auschwitz?

Steven   Auschwitz?

Barry   People in concentration camps. Those skull-like faces. All teeth and eye sockets.

Phone rings.

Steven *picks it up.*

Steven   Yes? . . . (*At* **Barry**.) Janis wants to know if you'd like some tea?

Barry   No, no, I'm fine.

Steven   He's fine . . . We're *both* fine . . . Eh? . . . Well, tell him Graffiti Busters is the best fucking cleaning firm in East London and in this business you get what you pay for. He wants to pay peanuts, he'll get monkeys.

Hangs up.

Barry   She's a good one – Janis.

Steven   Yes.

Barry   Best secretary you've ever had, I reckon. Next to . . . what was her name? Paulette?

Steven   Yes. Paulette was good.

Barry   So was Kelly.

Steven   Yes.

Barry   So was Maxine.

Steven   . . . Yes.

Barry   Your Debbie was the best, though.

Steven   Debbie was very good, yes.

Barry   No she wasn't.

Steven   No.

Barry   She makes a better wife than a secretary, eh?

Steven   . . . Yes.

Barry   She wasn't as bad in the office as me, though.
I'm hopeless.

Steven   You're not / hopeless at all.

Barry   I look at a computer – it crashes! I've been born in
the wrong time, I reckon. Wrong era. Few hundred years
ago – that would have suited me. Sort of Renaissance times.
That's more like *five* hundred years ago, isn't it?

Steven   I'm . . . not / sure when . . .

Barry   Wine out of goblets and candlelight and – Dad liked
candlelight, didn't he. Remember the candles in the shed?
The silver candelabrum!

Steven   Yes, yes.

Barry   I've got Dad's romantic DNA, I reckon. I should've
been mates with Byron and Shelley and all that lot. White
frilly shirts. Reading poetry all day. And making love all
night.

Steven   *And* catching syphilis.

Barry   They can cure that.

Steven   Not then. Your nose would drop off.

Barry   Who needs a nose? It's an affectation. Take it.

They laugh.

I like it when you laugh. Come here, brov.

Hugs **Steven**.

Barry   Fuck, you're all tense. I'll give you a massage.
Come on.

Steven   Not now.

Barry   Later?

Steven   Yes.

Barry   You won't let me forget now.

Steven   No.

Beat.

Barry   She showed me the picture.

Steven   Wh-what?

Barry   Debbie. Picture of the scan.

Steven   Oh!

Barry   The baby.

Steven   Yes, yes.

Barry   Beautiful. Little legs. Heart.

Steven   Barry . . . why did you run away from the job
this morning?

Barry   Oh. Right.

Beat.

We drove to the estate. Me and Jacko and Marky-boy.
They're still concentration camp victims. They keep talking
to me but I . . . I can't understand them. I recognise all the

words but . . . my brain – it can't work out the . . . the . . .
– Or perhaps it *won't*! Yes! That's it! Jacko and Marky-boy –
they're telling me what they went through in a concentration
camp and my brain's trying to protect me from –

Steven   Barry!

Barry   Yes, brov?

Steven   Tell me what happened this morning.

Barry   . . . A shaft of light.

Steven   What?

Barry   It breaks through the grey clouds like a . . . a . . .
Fuck knows. But it breaks through and it – Spotlight! It hits
the wall. The graffiti. And it . . . oh, brov, I see . . . I fucking
see . . .

Steven   What?

Barry   So much colour! All over the wall! It's so bright.
Like stained glass! Dazzling – You know the graffiti I'm
talking about.

Steven   I'm not sure if I –

Barry   *You* booked the job, Steve.

Steven   Well, yes, but I can't remember *every* –

Barry   *Try*, Steve. The graffiti in the estate. Huge wall.

Steven   . . . I might not've actually *seen* the –

Barry   You *did*. I *know* you did. *Try* to remember.

Beat.

Shall I give you a clue?

Steven   . . . Okay.

Barry   You want me to give you a clue?

Steven   Yes.

Barry   . . . An explosion.

Steven   An ex . . . plos . . . – *Oh!*

Barry   Go on!

Steven   Something to do with that . . . that bomb that went off.

Barry   Suicide bomber.

Steven   In the local market.

Barry   That's it!

Steven   Terrible.

Barry   A kid was killed.

Steven   Lucky there wasn't more.

Barry   Not lucky for the kid.

Steven   No.

Barry   He was just a boy. Ten.

Steven   Yes, yes, terrible.

Barry   The bomber wasn't much older.

Steven   Really?

Barry   Fifteen.

Steven   Really.

Barry   Just five years older.

Steven   I'd worked that out, yes.

Barry   They found his head in a supermarket trolley.

Steven   No!

Barry   . . . No. I made that bit up. Good image though.

Steven   'Good image'?!

Barry   Remember that interview with the bomber's mum?

Steven   I don't think I –

Barry   She said how her son was the most considerate child a mother could ever have in the whole world.

Steven   Goes to show.

Barry   What?

Steven   That . . . he wasn't.

Barry   Not really. He could still be the most considerate child in the whole world to his mum and a right evil bastard to everyone else, couldn't he.

Steven   . . . I suppose he could.

Barry   He was in the graffiti.

Steven   The bomber?

Barry   The kid who was killed.

Steven   Yes, yes, I remember now.

Barry   There was all this burning wreckage. The flames were all cadmium yellow and vermillion. And there was this crowd standing round watching it. And all the firelight was reflected in their faces. In their eyes. And out of the flames . . . the kid was rising up. And he had wings. He was an angel. And he was flying up to the sky. And the sky was all deep blue. Ultramarine. And there were hundreds of stars – Dad told us once stars were sort of doors . . . gateways to death. Remember that?

Steven   He . . . he didn't tell me.

Barry   He did. I was there.

Steven   He didn't.

Barry   He did.

Steven   Okay, okay, he did. But I've forgot.

Barry   You never listened to *anything* Dad said.

Steven   That's not true.

Barry   You never really spoke to him.

Steven   Of course I / spoke to him.

Barry   When you said anything, you always directed it at Mum. You wouldn't even *look* at Dad. Don't you regret behaving like that now? Eh? I know *I* would.

Beat.

Then –

That's why Van Gogh painted stars!

Steven   Eh? What?

Barry   Van Gogh. The painter.

Steven   Yes, yes, I know / who Van Gogh is.

Barry   He painted stars as if they were rainbow whirlpools. Everyone looks at them and goes, 'Ooo, how pretty.' And it's a sky full of death.

Steven   Barry. All I want to know is –

Barry   I couldn't clean away that graffiti, brov!

Steven   You . . . couldn't?

Barry   All the colour. The shapes. It'd be a fucking sin.

Steven   'A *sin*'?!

Barry   Why'd they wanna get rid of it anyway? It's a tribute.

Steven   People felt it was . . . morally ambiguous.

Barry   'Morally ambiguous'?! Where the fuck is the moral fucking ambiguity? One kid exploded a bomb. One didn't. One guilty. One innocent. Nothing 'ambiguous' there. Or am I missing something? Eh? Tell me.

Steven   I think some people thought the boy rising from the flames . . . it could be mistaken for the suicide bomber and that . . . even if it wasn't . . . it could be seen as . . . glorifying . . . you know.

Barry   No. What?

Steven   Death.

Barry   I ran.

Steven   Y-you . . .?

Barry   I yelled at Jacko and Marky-boy, 'I will *not* fucking destroy that work of art! Fuck Graffiti Busters! I won't do it! I won't! *I won't!*'

Phone rings.

Steven *picks it up.*

Steven   . . . Everything's fine . . . Eh? . . . That's the estimate, yes . . . Well, tell them Graffiti Busters is the best fucking cleaning firm in East London and in this business you get what you pay for. They want to pay peanuts, they'll get monkeys.

Hangs up.

Barry   Your mind. It's like a . . . a laser. You know that? It's full of all that . . . energy. If your brain was an animal, you know what it'd be? Eh? A shark. Sharks have to keep swimming otherwise they die. Sharks never sleep. That's what they say, anyway. Imagine that, brov. We're living in a world where there are no dreaming sharks.

Steven   . . . Take a few days off.

Barry   I want to quit, Steve.

Steven   Wh-what? When?

Barry   Now.

Steven   No.

Barry   It's not fair on you.

Steven   Don't worry about me.

Barry   This is *your* business.

Steven   *Our* business.

Barry   What the fuck did *I* do?

Steven   A lot.

Barry   Nothing. *You* built it up. From scratch. My brother – The Man With The Plan.

Steven   You're *part* of that plan.

Barry   I'm a joke.

Steven   No.

Barry   The way people look at me.

Steven   *How* do they look?

Barry   Charity case.

Steven   *No one* / thinks that.

Barry   You've always known how to make money.

Steven   I . . . I've worked / hard, yes.

Barry   . . . I know you feel it, Steve.

Steven   I . . . what?

Barry   Me and you. We're . . . drifting.

Steven   Drifting?

Barry   Icebergs.

Steven   'Ice . . .'?

Barry   Fuck, Steve. It's about time. That's all I'm saying.

Steven   I don't know what you –

Barry   We've got to talk about it.

Steven   . . . About *what*?

Barry   Jesus, Steve, *don't*.

Steven   Every time you fuck up you give me this . . . this . . .

Barry   This, this?

Steven   Like it's . . . my fault.

Barry   Do you *think* it's *your* fault?

Steven   You tell me.

Barry   No. *You* tell *me*.

Steven   No. You tell –

Barry   *You* should be the one to start talking about it. *You're* the one who fucking *did* it, Steve. *You!*

Steven   *What* did I fucking do?

Beat.

What *is* it you think I did?

6

Steven   I remember . . . I'm fifteen years old. I'm in the back garden. Dark. Cold. I'm looking through the window into Dad's shed. The candles are flickering. Dad's sorting through his notebooks. He's got lots of little notebooks. They're full of his scribbles and doodles. That's what he calls them. 'Oh, these are just my scribbles and doodles.' He's been keeping the notebooks for years. Since he was a kid. Dad's notebooks are private. He keeps them in an old biscuit tin. There's a picture on the top. Snow. A frozen lake. Dad picks up the notebooks. All of them. He walks out of the shed. He doesn't see me. He goes over to a big metal drum. He drops the notebooks into it. He piles bits of wood on top. He strikes a match. He holds the match above the big metal drum. He's going to drop the match into it. I want to cry out, 'Dad! What're you doing? That's all your scribbles and doodles you're going to burn!' But I don't and . . . – Whoosh! Flames. Everything is burning. I look at Dad. There's lots of sparks all round his head. I remember thinking . . . they look like stars.

7

Steven *and* **Debbie***'s house.*

Steven *and* **Debbie** *are eating dinner.*

Debbie   My sister saw a UFO.

Steven   Really?

Debbie   She was in some playground somewhere.

Steven   Oh?

Debbie   Her and this new bloke of hers. They climbed over this fence or whatever and got inside. Night.

Steven   She'll get in trouble one day.

Debbie   Is the lamp too bright?

Steven   I . . . I don't know.

Debbie   Think it might be.

Steven   Perhaps a bit.

Debbie *turns lamp off.*

Debbie   Better?

Steven   Much.

Debbie   Cleo says they had a twirl on the whatnot then flopped in the sandpit.

Steven   Didn't think playgrounds *had* sandpits anymore.

Debbie   Oh?

Steven   Danger hazard.

Debbie   '*Danger* hazard'?

Steven   Dog poo.

Debbie   Eating, Steven, eating.

Steven   Sorry.

They eat . . .

Then –

When *was* this?

Debbie   What?

Steven   The UFO.

Debbie   Oh. Last week sometime, I think.

Steven   *You* went out with her last week.

Debbie   I know I did.

Steven   Twice. Till late.

Debbie   So?

Steven   So . . . Cleo goes out a lot.

Debbie   She likes to have fun. She likes to . . . to go wild now and again. She'd end up in a fucking straitjacket otherwise.

They eat . . .

Then –

Is it a bit dark now?

Steven   I . . . whatever you think.

Debbie   Can you see your food?

Steven   Yes.

Debbie   You *can*?

Steven   Can't you?

They eat . . .

Then –

Debbie   Anyway, they were gazing up at the sky. In this danger hazard of a sandpit. In each other's arms. It was all very romantic. Horny. You know? Bloody horny?

Steven   . . . Yes.

Debbie   And then . . . then they see something in the sky. Right above them.

Steven   Jesus!

Debbie   I know. Cleo said there weren't any flashing lights or anything.

Steven   Really?

Debbie   Nothing like the films.

Steven   Really?

Debbie   And she said it was dead quiet.

Steven   Jesus.

Debbie   I know. She said the UFO was just this round shaped . . . Darkness.

Steven   Darkness!?

Debbie   What the fuck's wrong with you?

Steven   . . . Sorry?

Debbie   Stop being so fucking . . . interested.

Steven   But I *am* interested.

Debbie   Are you?

Steven   Yes.

Debbie   *Are* you?

Steven   . . . Yes.

Slight pause.

Debbie   I can't see my food.

Turns lamp on.

They eat . . .

Then –

Steven   When did you show Barry the photo?

Debbie   Eh? What?

Steven   Barry said you showed him the photo of the scan.

Debbie   I . . . yes, I did.

Steven   When?

Debbie   I don't know. Day before yesterday.

Steven   He came round?

Debbie   Yes.

Steven   Out of the blue?

Debbie   No. You *asked* him to.

Steven   I didn't.

Debbie   You did. I heard you on the phone.

Steven   No.

Debbie   You asked him to clear some space in the cellar.

Steven   'Space in the –'?

Debbie   For your mum's stuff! The stuff we're storing when she moves. Remember?

Steven   Oh . . .

Debbie   Oh!

Beat.

They eat . . .

Then –

I'm sure we've got rats.

Steven   Where?

Debbie   In the cellar.

Steven   No.

Debbie   Well, I heard *something*.

Steven   Not rats.

Debbie   I had enough of rats when I was a kid. Afraid to let my feet poke out of the bed covers in case my toes got nibbled off.

Beat.

This light's giving me a fucking headache!

Turns lamp off.

That better? For you? What d'you think? This –?

Turns lamp on.

Or this?

Turns lamp off.

This?

Lamp on.

Or this?

Off.

This?

On.

Or this?

Off.

This?

On.

Or this?

Off.

8

Liz's *house.*

Steve *and* **Barry**.

Barry *drops box.*

Steven   Jesus!

Barry   Sorry.

Steven   You've got to be careful, Barry.

Barry   It slipped.

Steven   Why don't you sit down for a while.

Barry   I want to help.

Steven   Make us all a cup of tea.

Barry   *You* make us all a cup of tea. I'm not in your office now.

Liz *walks in, holding box.*

Liz   What was that noise?

Steven   Nothing.

Barry   I dropped this.

Liz   Oh, no.

Goes to box.

What with half my stuff in your brother's cellar and you breaking everything else, I'm not gonna have much to take with me, am I?

Steven   You'll have plenty, Mum.

Liz   It'll *look* like plenty cos I'm squeezing a two-bedroom house into a pokey flat.

Steven   It's not pokey.

Beat.

(*At* **Barry**.) Did you tell Mum about our old room, brov?

Barry   Eh?

Steven   The wall.

Barry   Oh. No.

Steven   He peeled off some wallpaper, Mum.

Liz   Really?

Steven   There was some writing on the wall underneath.

Barry   *I* did it.

Steven   When he was . . . *how* old? Nine or something?

Barry   Younger.

Steven   Guess what is was, Mum.

Liz   What –? Oh, how can I?

Steven *and* **Barry**   'Steven and Barry Forever.'

Steven *and* **Barry** *laugh.*

Barry   Mum. Don't you think he's got a great smile?

Liz   He's got his Dad's smile.

Steven   I haven't got / Dad's smile.

Liz   You've got your dad's smile and Barry's got mine.

Barry   That's right.

Steven   I have *not* got Dad's smile.

Barry   Then whose smile *have* you got?

Steven   Wh-why do I have to have *anyone's* smile? Why can't I just have *my* smile?

Barry (*at* **Liz**)   What's he going on about?

Liz   Don't ask me! I've never understood half of what he – Oh, no! Look!

Has taken a (smashed) framed photo out of a box.

Steven   Careful, you'll cut yourself.

Liz   I know.

Barry   It's only the glass that's broke.

Steven   The photo's okay.

Barry   You can get it re-framed.

Steven   I'll get it done for you.

Liz   This was the last picture your dad took of you both. Remember?

Steven   No.

Barry   *I* do. We're in the garden.

Steven   Well, I can tell that much.

Barry   It's my tenth birthday. That T-shirt. I drew those stars on it. Remember? With those special pens Dad bought for me.

Liz   We *both* bought them for you.

Barry   Each star's a different colour. See? Took me ages. Dad loved it. Said I should start a stall and sell them. Taught me the sales pitch and everything. 'Barry's T-Shirts! Covered in stars! Each one a different colour!' Remember?

Steven   No.

Barry   I wore that T-shirt all the time after Dad . . . after he died.

Liz   . . . You used to be such a beautiful boy, Barry.

Beat.

Steven   . . . Brov, why don't you put the box in my car?

Throws car keys to **Barry**.

Beat.

Barry *goes.*

Steven   He's trying his best, Mum.

Liz   If you say so.

Steven   He's not drunk anything for three months.

Liz   He'll start again.

Steven   No. He *means* it this time.

Liz   He's meant it all the other times. Every other time since he was thirteen.

Steven   He didn't have a drink problem when he was thirteen.

Liz   I imagined the piles of vomit I had to clean up, did I?

Steven   You weren't cleaning them up when he was *thirteen*, Mum.

Liz   Don't tell me what vomit I did and did not clean up. And he was at it younger than thirteen. Twelve. Eleven.

Steven   You're being stupid now.

Liz   What about that time he nearly demolished the house?

Steven   'Nearly demolished –?'

Liz   He smashed all those things you bought me.

Steven   *What* things?

Liz   Ornaments. Glass.

Steven   Glass . . .?

Liz   Barry smashed them all. Every one. We were finding bits of glass in the carpet for years.

Beat.

Barry would be such a disappointment to your dad.

Steven   Don't, Mum.

Liz   Well, it's true. Dad *adored* Barry. You *know* that.

Beat.

Steven   He's hoping to have another exhibition, you know.

Liz   *Another?* When was the first?

Steven   That thing down Bethnal Green Road.

Liz   Drawings Blu Tacked on a wall?

Steven   They *weren't* Blu Tacked.

Liz   Well, it wasn't an exhibition.

Steven   It was part of a student show, Mum.

Liz   'Student'? Barry?!

Steven   He got into Goldsmith's.

Liz   And lasted all of seven weeks.

Steven   Oh, it was longer than that.

Liz   Not *much* longer.

Steven   But he *did* get in.

Liz   It's not the *getting* in that matters in life, Steven. It's the *staying* in.

Beat.

Ted took me to see an exhibition once.

Steven   Ted?

Liz   From the fruit and veg stall.

Steven   Oh. Him.

Liz   Don't say it like that.

Steven   Like what?

Liz   He treated me lovely. He paid for a taxi all the way there.

Steven   Where?

Liz   This . . . art gallery. Some big building down Piccadilly. *You* know where I mean.

Steven   I *don't*.

Liz   You *do*! Water lilies. That's what the paintings were of. Dreamy. Like looking into that aquarium at the dentists. Now *that's* what I call an exhibition. Not Blu Tacked . . . I can't even think of a word to describe what Barry did.

Steven   They were images of war, Mum.

Liz   They were revolting. Who'd want one of those on the living room wall?

Steven   I don't think they were *meant* to –

Liz   You think it was easy for me? Eh? Seeing my son do stuff like that? Knowing it came out of his head? Well, *do* you?

Steven   . . . No.

Beat.

Liz   You remember what Barry was like before your dad died, Steven? So clever. Always interested. Asking questions and . . . laughing. He used to laugh all the time.

Steven   I wish you wouldn't keep going / over all of this.

Liz   After your dad died, he was nothing but trouble.

Steven   . . . Grief affects people in different ways, I suppose.

Liz   It was the *making* of you.

Steven   Don't say that.

Liz   It was. You blossomed.

Steven   No! I . . . I didn't . . . I . . .

Liz   What's wrong? You're shaking.

Steven   You make it sound like I . . . Jesus!

Liz Steve?

Steven Just because I didn't go around crying all the bloody time. Just because I didn't get pissed and – I *loved* Dad!

Liz I *know* you did.

Steven I *still* do.

Liz Of *course* you –

Steven I *still* love him! *Still! Still!*

9

Steven I'm in my bedroom. Barry's making a noise. He's in his side of the room but he's still bugging me. He's pinned a large sheet of paper on the wall. He's using coloured pencils to draw something. A leaf. Bright red. He found it on the way home from school. 'Look at this! Look at this!' He was all giggly and excited the way he gets. And now he's drawing it – Huge! Every little vein and . . . insect bite. Barry's making those little gaspy noises. He's facing the wall. He's got his back to me. He picks up a pencil . . . Orange. He shades the leaf some more. Little gasps. I can't see his face but I know he'll be licking his fucking lips. Lick, lick. I look at the pencils. Some are very sharp. I want to stab him in the neck with one. I want to really hurt him. Barry looks at me and says, 'Nearly finished. Dad's gonna love it. What d'you think, Steve?' I look at his drawing. Barry's waiting for an answer. I wonder what he'd do if I stuck a pencil in each fucking eye. Pop. Pop. I walk out of the room without saying anything and – There's Dad! He's downstairs. By the front door. His hand is on it like he's about to go out but . . . he's not wearing a coat. And he's got his slippers on. He can't be going out dressed like *that*. Dad opens the front door and a gust of air blows up the stairs. So cold. I hear Barry call, 'Dad!' from the bedroom. He's finished the drawing. He wants Dad to tell him how brilliant it is. Dad looks up the stairs. He sees me. I know if I tell Dad not to go out – or if I

smile even, smile just a little – Dad will stay. But I don't say
anything. I don't smile. Not even a little. I just stare at Dad.
Dad leaves the house and closes the door behind him. Barry
comes out of the bedroom. 'Where's Dad?' 'He's gone out,' I
tell him. 'He said he'd rather go out in the freezing cold than
see another one of your stupid fucking drawings.' Barry
starts crying. He runs back into the bedroom. I listen to him
cry. I'm not angry with him anymore. I'm not in a bad mood
about anything. I feel very calm.

10

Barry's *flat*.

Steven *and* **Barry**.

Steven *is in a neck brace and holding a walking stick*.

Barry   First surprise!

Steven   Okay.

Barry   Don't look.

Steven   I won't.

Barry   Eyes closed.

Steven   Yes, yes.

Barry *reveals painting of devastated landscape*.

Barry   Okay . . . Open.

Steven *opens his eyes*.

Barry   Well?

Steven   Wow!

Slight pause.

It's big.

Barry   Is it?

Steven   Well . . . it's bigger than . . .

Barry   Something smaller?

Steven   . . . Yes.

Barry   I call it *Love Song for the Offspring of Enola Gay*.

Steven   . . . Intriguing.

Barry   Know who Enola Gay was?

Steven   Some pop group or / something?

Barry   Hiroshima.

Steven   That.

Barry   The pilot of the aircraft – the aircraft that was gonna drop the bomb . . . forget his name. Don't matter . . . This bomb – it's the biggest ever fuck-off bomb ever made, right? Everyone in the world knows. They've done the tests, for chrissakes. In that desert. The explosion was so hot the sand – it was turned to glass. You know that, brov?

Steven   No.

Barry   . . . This fucking bomb . . . this fucking fuck-off bomb – whole islands were destroyed. You've seen that, haven't you? Boom! Boiled fish in the water. Nuclear fallout whatsit like snow. Sunsets like fucking . . . blood. Like the fucking sky had cut its wrists. And hey! I should know eh?

Steven   Don't joke about that, Barry.

Barry   And pigs. They put pigs on ships near to the islands. Know why? To see what the bomb would do to them. Turned them into pork scratchings, that's what! So . . . everyone *knew* what this bomb could do, right? This pilot who's gonna drop the bomb – *he* knows. This bomb is one evil fucker. And the pilot has to think of a name for the plane. You with me?

Steven   Yes, yes.

Barry   So what does he call it. 'Evil Fucker With Fuck-Off Bomb'? 'Wings of Terror'? No. He calls it 'Enola Gay'. And you know who Enola Gay was?

Steven   No.

Barry   His mother.

Stumbles.

Steven   Careful.

Barry   I'm not drunk.

Steven   I know.

Barry   Haven't had a mouthful. Sixteen weeks.

Steven   I'm proud of you.

Barry   You'd be annoyed if I started again, wouldn't you?

Steven   I'd be . . . upset.

Barry   Annoyed.

Steven   Disappointed.

Barry   You'd want to hit me probably.

Steven   No.

Barry   You *would*.

Steven   I *wouldn't*.

Barry   Why don't you whack me in the face with your stick? Go on! Knock a few teeth out.

Beat.

Next surprise!

Steven   Okay.

Barry   Don't look!

Steven   I won't.

Barry   Eyes closed?

Steven   Yes, yes.

Barry *puts on a crash helmet.*

Barry   Open.

Steven   Wow!

Barry   Why am I wearing this, d'you think?

Steven   . . . You haven't bought a –?

Barry   Look out the window.

Steven *hesitates.*

Barry   Go on!

Steven *goes to window.*

Barry   Surprise!

Steven   Expensive.

Barry   Very.

Steven   How?

Barry   Put the two surprises together.

Steven   You . . . you sold the painting!

Barry   A dealer from Manchester. She thinks I'm brilliant.
She wants that painting, the three over there – when they're
finished – and . . .

Opens a portfolio.

These drawings. They're a sequence. You see? Individually
they don't make much sense. Composition's all fucked up.

Steven   I wouldn't know.

Barry   Trust me. Fucked up. But when you put them next
to each other and . . . it'll start to balance out. Make sense.
The same images occur in all of them. You see? A house . . . a
tree –

Steven   Aww!

Clutches his knee.

Barry   Fuck! I should've offered you a seat. Sorry.

Steven   Just a twinge.

Barry   My brother the hero! – Here!

Steven *sits.*

Barry   I feel terrible now. You come all the way round here to see me. And all I do is ramble on and on about myself and – Why didn't you tell me to shut the fuck up?

Steven   I like to hear you talk.

Barry   I haven't even asked how you're feeling.

Steven   Don't worry about it.

Barry   I *am* worried.

Beat.

Steve?

Steven   Yes, brov?

Barry   How're you feeling?

Steven   A lot better. Thank you.

Barry   Any pain in the neck?

Steven   No, no. All cleared up.

Barry   Why're you still wearing that, then?

Indicates neck brace.

Steven   Just in case.

Barry   In case what?

Steven   In case . . .

Beat.

Barry How's the bruising?

Steven   All gone.

Barry So it's just . . . what? The knee?

Steven   Only when I've been standing for too long.

Barry I'm a thoughtless bastard.

Steven   No, no.

Barry I am, I am. I was just eager to show you –

Steven   I know, I know. And I was eager to see!

Barry Shall I get my healing crystal?

Steven   Oh . . . I . . .

Barry It'll help.

Steven   No, it's fine.

Barry It'll help.

Steven   . . . Go on, then.

Barry *gets crystal.*

He places it on **Steven***'s knee.*

Barry How's that feel?

Steven   Mmm.

Barry Can you feel the energy?

Steven   I'm not sure . . .

Barry Does it feel warm? Bet it does.

Steven   . . . It does a bit.

Barry That's the healing energy.

Steven   Really?

Barry Really.

Beat.

Debbie said your memory's come back.

Steven What?

Barry About the crash.

Steven Oh. Yes.

Barry You swerved to avoid a kid who'd ran out?

Steven A boy, yes. And he . . . he didn't run out.

Barry Oh?

Steven He was just sort of . . . there.

Barry There?

Steven In the middle of the road – Has Debbie told you all this?

Barry No, no.

Steven I turned a corner and – There he is!

Barry Fuck me!

Steven In my car headlights. Just staring.

Barry You've been seeing too many horror films.

Steven It's not a joke.

Barry . . . I know. Sorry. Crashing into a wall is serious.

Steven Corrugated iron.

Barry What?

Steven It wasn't a wall. It was a fence.

Barry Of corrugated iron.

Steven Yes.

Barry . . . It *could've* been a wall.

Steven It could've. But it wasn't.

Barry But if it was a wall . . . ooo, shudder, shudder. Eh, brov? You might've beaten me to it. Driving straight into a wall – Splat! Better than me and my wrists. We'll both have to work harder at it, though. Can't keep bodging it, can we, brov? Eh?

Beat.

Steven . . . When did you speak to her?

Barry Who?

Steven Debbie. She told you my memory was coming back, you said.

Barry . . . Debbie said you get pissed off when I talk to her.

Steven I am *not* pissed off.

Barry You are.

Steven I'm just curious.

Barry I can feel the crystal getting really hot.

Steven So . . . when did you . . .?

Barry Mmm?

Steven See Debbie.

Barry When I went round.

Steven To the house?

Barry Yeah.

Steven When?

Barry Eh?

Steven When did you go round?

Barry To *your* place?

Steven Yes. Yes!

Barry   Ooo . . . I forget – Bloody hell, can you feel it, brov?
Energy!

Steven   *Why* did you go round, Barry?

Barry   Round where?

Steven   To the house!

Barry   If you get wound up it'll divert the healing flow.

Steven   I am not getting wound up. I just want to know
why you went round the bloody house.

Barry   Mum couldn't find something. Thought it might be
in your cellar. I popped round to have a look.

Steven   *What* couldn't she find?

Barry   I forget now.

Steven   Why didn't Mum ask *me* to look for whatever it was?

Barry   She did.

Steven   She didn't.

Barry   Lots of times, she said.

Steven   No.

Barry   Perhaps it was one of the things you forgot.

Steven   I remember *everything* now.

Barry   You do?

Steven   Yes!

Barry   There's only one explanation, then.

Steven   What?

Barry   Mum's a lying, two-faced, manipulative old cow.

Beat.

Steven   . . . Mum could've phoned Debbie.

Barry   Debbie won't go down the cellar. Not with the rats.

Steven   We have *not got rats* – Okay, okay, enough!

Stands.

Barry   It feels better, don't it?

Steven   What I don't understand is why . . . why Debbie never tells me when she sees you. Why it always slips out accidently.

Barry   'Slips out accidently'?

Steven   Are you fucking her, Barry?

Beat.

Then –

Barry *laughs.*

Steven   Don't fucking laugh. Something . . . something's going on. I know there is. They're whispering at work.

Barry   *'Whispering'?!*

Steven   Why'd it take her so long to tell me she was pregnant? What was she waiting for? Debating whether to have it or not? Because it's *not* mine. Because it's *yours!*

Barry *laughs louder.*

Steven   Shut up! Shut up!

Starts ripping up drawings.

Barry   No! Steve!

Tries to stop him.

For fuck's sake!

Steven *calms.*

Slight pause.

Steven   I'm . . . I'm sorry.

Barry   Fuck off.

Steven   Are they okay?

Barry   Do they *look* okay?

Steven   I'll pay you for them.

Barry   Oh, that's your fucking answer for everything! *Money!*

Steven   No.

Barry   Money! Money!

Steven's *phone rings.*

Steven   Hello . . . Eh? What? . . . To do it properly five days . . . Well, whatever we said . . . Tell him Graffiti Busters is the best fucking . . . cleaning . . . you get what you . . . pay . . . pay for . . . I can't think now, Jan. I'm sorry. I . . . I can't.

Hangs up.

Beat.

Barry   It'll be fine, brov. I can do them again.

Steven   You sure?

Barry   I'll do them better. They'll be brilliant.

Beat.

Steven   I don't know why I said –

Barry   I know.

Steven   You . . . you won't tell Debbie?

Barry   Of course not.

Steven   I don't want her to think –

Barry   I can keep a secret. You *know* that. Lips sealed.

11

Steven*'s house. Night.*

Steven *holds walking stick. No neck brace.*

A television is blaring.

Debbie *enters.*

Debbie   Steve?

Beat.

What the fuck's going on?

Turns television off.

It's the middle of the bloody night – Oh, no! Look!

Sees red stain on white rug.

What's got into you lately? Everything you bloody touch . . .
Broke. Smashed. That clock my sister gave us. Still don't
know how I'm gonna tell her. All those little shiny things
inside. All spinning and whirling. Not anymore.

Steven *is pouring drink.*

Debbie   Jesus! What you drinking for?

Steven   Why'd we buy the fucking stuff if we weren't gonna
drink it?

Debbie   We bought it cos it goes with the cocktail cabinet.

Steven   Why'd we buy the fucking cabinet, then?

Debbie   We liked the way it lights up.

Steven   *You* liked the way it lights up!

Debbie   So did *you*.

Steven   No. I *never* liked it. I don't think I like one fucking
thing in this whole fucking house. I don't like the leather
sofa and the glass coffee table and the glass shelves – Why's
there so much fucking glass anyway? It's like living in a . . . a
. . . I dunno. Greenhouse! Ice palace!

Debbie   This'll stain, you know.

Indicates rug.

Steven   Another polar bear skinned in vain.

Debbie   It's not polar bear.

Steven   Tell you what, I'll drive you to London Zoo one night. You can scale the fence and club a bear over the head. Use one of your five hundred handbags. That gold crocodile skin monstrosity that cost a fortune. You can fill it with all the jewellery you've been buying since we got married and – Whack! One dead polar bear.

Debbie   You finished?

Steven   Or . . . or . . . you can kill it by feeding it one of your chicken nugget risottos. Or make it listen to you droning on about your hard-luck fucking childhood and the way you always dreamed of . . . what was it again? A house with a swimming pool and barbeques every Sunday and lazing with girlfriends nibbling cheesecake and sipping Chardonnay –

Debbie   I've *never* said I wanted that!

Steven   YOU FUCKING DID!

Raises walking stick –

Debbie   OH, *REALLY?*

Snatches walking stick from him as –

REALLY?

Strikes his injured knee with walking stick.

Steven *cries out and falls.*

Debbie *throws the walking stick at him as –*

Debbie   You pathetic bastard!

Steven *is clutching his leg, whimpering . . .*

Debbie   What *is* it, Steve? Eh? *What?* The past few months you've been . . . My sister *said* I should say something. Have it out with him she said. I *should've* done.

Steven   Why *didn't* you, then?

Debbie   I'm eight months pregnant!

Steven   You think I don't fucking *know* that?!

Debbie   Are you seeing Janis?

Steven   Wh-what?

Debbie   Are you having sex with Janis?

Steven   No!

Debbie   Well, it's *her* you've been calling late at night. I checked your phone.

Steven   You . . . you checked / my phone –

Debbie   Of *course* I fucking did!

Steven   . . . Jesus . . . Jesus . . .

Debbie   . . . I phoned your office last week. They told me you were out at lunch. I knew where you were. *La Forchetta*.

Steven   You're having me followed!

Debbie   It's where you *always* go! You'd be sitting where you always sit. The table by the window. You'd be cleaning your knife and fork with the serviette. Then you'd straighten the tablecloth and ask the waitress for a Diet Coke with ice and lemon. You'd spend ages looking at the menu and then order what you always order. Veal Escalope al Limone with side order of peas. 'Any garlic bread, sir?' You'd think about it for a moment, frowning, then say what you always say. 'No'. When the meal arrives you'll have black pepper but only on the veal please. You'll cut the meat into exactly the same-sized little bits. You won't look at the person sitting opposite you. Not once. You won't ask how their meal is. You won't tell them how yours is. When you've finished you'll move your empty plate to another table immediately and gaze out of the window. You'll ask for the dessert menu but in the end you settle for just a cappuccino. Then you'll go to the bathroom and clean your teeth with that little airport toothbrush you keep in your breast pocket. Then you'll suck a peppermint so strong it makes your eyes water. Then you'll come back to the table and pay with your credit card and leave a ten per cent tip worked out to the last bloody decimal point. Then you'll say, 'No rest for the wicked' and rush back to the office. At some point on the way back you'll mention how you've eaten too much and need to 'join a gym and get in shape.' And the person you're with will say, 'You look in pretty good shape to me.' Like I used to. Although now, of course, it's not me. It's Janis.

Beat.

Steven   I'm seeing a ghost.

Debbie   . . . *What?*

Steven   A ghost, Debbie. I'm seeing a ghost.

Debbie *stares.*

Steven   I've . . . I've seen it a few times.

Debbie   Oh! *So this* is your excuse, is it?

Steven   It's *not* an excuse.

Debbie   Cleo said you'll come out with some pathetic / bullshit like you always –

Steven   *Look* at me! Does it *look* like I'm making it up?

Debbie   You look like my dad used to! When he came home from one of his sluts! Guilty!

Beat.

Steven   . . . A few weeks ago, on the way back from Barry's, I stopped off at the supermarket. You asked to get me some things – Bleach! Olive oil! Remember?

Debbie   No. But go on. I'm intrigued.

Steven   . . . It was late. The supermarket was practically empty. I turned into an aisle and – There he was!

Debbie   . . . Who?

Steven   The child.

Debbie   *What* fucking child?

Steven   The boy I nearly hit with the car. He was just standing there. Staring at me. Wearing the same T-shirt as when I saw him in the road. I looked round to see who was with and when I looked back . . . he was gone. I looked up and down every aisle. He had just . . . disappeared.

Beat.

A few days later I went to check on some work Marky-boy was doing. An alleyway somewhere and – There he was again. Wearing the same T-shirt. Standing right beside Marky-boy. I called out, 'Who's the kid?' Marky-boy said, 'What kid?' Marky-boy couldn't see him. That's when I realised . . . the boy in the T-shirt – he was a ghost.

Beat.

I told Janis because I / remember her telling me –

Debbie   Janis! We get there at last!

Steven   Her husband died of some blood clot thing – aneurysm.

Debbie   You'll say anything, won't you? / You'll just lie and lie and . . .

Steven   She told me how she used to . . . to feel his presence in the flat where they lived. Sometimes Jan used to hear her husband's fingernails scraping the side of the armchair. Like he used to when he watched television. That's what got Jan into Spiritualism. That's what I've been talking to her about. Ghosts.

Beat.

Debbie *goes to pick up rug –*

Steven   Deb! Janis said this ghost I'm seeing – this boy –
he's a tortured soul or something. He can't move on. He
needs my help.

Debbie *picks up rug and goes to leave –*

Steven   Deb! Listen to me! *Listen!*

Debbie *turns to face* **Steven**.

Steven   . . . Tonight I . . . I couldn't sleep. I . . . I came
down here. I turned the telly on. I poured a drink and –
Then I saw it.

Debbie   What?

Steven   The boy. He was standing there.

Points close to **Debbie**.

Debbie   Stop it, Steve.

Steven   I screamed. Dropped my drink –

Debbie   Don't!

Goes to leave again.

Steven   *Please*, Deb.

Debbie *stares at him.*

Steven   You've got to believe me.

Debbie *goes to say something . . . then lets it go.*

She walks out of the room.

Steven (*calling after her*)   Don't tell Barry. When you see him
. . . your little secret meetings . . . DON'T TELL HIM
ABOUT THE GHOST! DON'T TELL HIM ABOUT THE
GHOST! DON'T TELL HIM ABOUT –

12

Steven 'Ice!' Someone mentioned ice. I'm sitting at the top of the stairs. Barry's sitting next to me. He's crying and he's clutching the banisters – 'Frozen!' Something's been frozen. I peer between the banisters. The front door's open. Snow outside. People going in and out. Treading slush into the house. Down the hall. Into the living room. Mum won't like that. I can hear Mum crying. I can see shadows moving in the front room. Boots. Strange boots. I can hear walkie-talkies crackle. Police. I want to rush down but I know I mustn't. I've got to keep out of the way. The whole house feels different. It's three days since Dad went missing – 'Peaceful!' What's peaceful? I know all these words have something to do with Dad. Every time one of them is said Mum cries louder. Keep listening . . . Victoria Park . . . Canal . . . Dad has been found now. He's been found in the canal by Victoria Park. The canal has frozen over. Dad is in the ice. He looks peaceful.

13

Liz's *new flat.*

Steven *and* **Liz.**

Steven *no longer has walking stick.*

Liz It's just that everything is so new. The houses, the street, the shops. It's like they've just been unpacked . . . Steven?

Steven What –? Oh, sorry, Mum.

Liz You sure you're okay?

Steven Yes, yes, I told you.

Liz I would say I don't like the neighbourhood. But you've got to have *neighbours* to have a *neighbourhood*. I don't see a soul. Don't *hear* a soul – Tell a lie! I heard a car door slam the other morning. There's no litter anywhere. No blobs of chewing gum on the pavement. It's all so polished and . . . There's no cracks to hold on to. I'm slipping off all the time. I should *never* have let you persuade me to leave my house.

Steven *What?!*

Liz On and on about the dog.

Steven *Me?*

Liz 'I'll get you somewhere new. I'll pay the rent. You won't have to do a thing.'

Steven I was trying to *help*, Mum.

Liz 'You'll never have any peace if you stay here.'

Steven I *never* said that.

Liz You did.

Steven No. I didn't.

Liz You . . . did.

Steven No! I bloody *didn't*!

Beat.

Mum . . . sit down. Please.

Liz What?

Steven I've got something to tell you.

Liz What's wrong?

Steven Nothing. I just . . . I just want to tell you something before you . . . before you hear it from someone else.

Liz You're making me nervous now.

Steven Sit down!

Liz *sits.*

Beat.

Steven   . . . Debbie thinks we've got rats.

Liz   Rats?

Steven   In the cellar.

Liz   Your house is brand new.

Steven   I know.

Liz   It's lovely. Expensive. You're rich.

Steven   I'm not rich.

Liz   You're rich. Don't be embarrassed by it – Droppings?

Steven   Eh?

Liz   Rat shit? You *seen* it?

Steven   No. I'm . . . well, I'm not sure.

Liz   Dropping are the first sign you've got –

Steven   Mum! Listen!

Liz   I *am* listening!

Steven   Debbie don't want to risk staying in the house.

Liz   . . . Oh.

Steven   She's nervous about stuff like that. With the baby
on the way.

Liz   . . . I see.

Steven   Infections.

Liz   Oh . . . yes.

Steven   So she's . . . she's gone to live with her sister for a
while.

Liz   When?

Steven   . . . Last night.

Liz   I see.

Steven   Just till I get it sorted out. The rats. That's if we *have* rats. Which I don't think we have.

Liz   But Debbie does?

Steven   . . . Yes.

Beat.

Liz   Well . . . you best sort it out quick then.

Steven   Yes, of course.

Liz   You don't want the mother of your child living somewhere else.

Steven   Of course not.

Liz   And I certainly don't want to schlep all the way to Debbie's sister's every time I want to see my grandchild – Where does she live again?

Steven   New Cross.

Liz   Take me all bloody day.

Steven   It won't come to that.

Liz   I should hope not.

Beat.

Can you cope?

Steven   What?

Liz   The cooking? The cleaning?

Steven   I can look after myself, Mum.

Liz   I was still doing your washing when you met Debbie.

Steven   Mum. I can load a washing machine.

Beat.

Liz   I remember when I first saw Debbie. I paid you a surprise visit in the office. Remember that? I was on the way to the cinema down Mile End with Jerry.

Steven   Jerry?

Liz   From the decorating shop.

Steven   Oh.

Liz   Striking woman, I thought. Debbie. I knew there was something going on between you both. You denied it. But you can't lie to me.

Steven   I didn't lie.

Liz   I'm your mother, Steve.

Steven   Debbie had only been there a few days when you first saw her.

Liz   There was *still* something going on. At least from her. I thought, she's older. But that's not a bad thing. I was older than your dad. Not as much as you and Debbie though.

Steven   It's only five years, Mum.

Liz   'Only'? Tell that to Debbie.

Sound of bike pulling up.

Oh! That's your brother.

Steven   You . . . you didn't tell me he was coming round.

Liz   I didn't know. *He* don't make appointments.

Goes to door.

Barry (*off*)   Hello, Mum.

Liz (*off*)   Hello, love.

Barry (*off*)   Steve here?

Liz (*off*)   Yes, yes.

Barry *enters.*

Barry   Hello.

Steven   Hello.

Liz   Do you wanna cup of tea, love?

Barry   Thanks, Mum.

Liz   Want another cup, Steve?

Steven   No.

Liz   'No thank you, Mum.'

Steven   No thank you, Mum.

Liz *goes to kitchen.*

Barry   Debbie said you'd probably be here.

Steven   Did she?

Barry   I've been phoning you all morning.

Steven   Oh?

Barry   Debbie said she's left you.

Beat.

She said you hit her.

Beat.

Well?

Steven   Of course I fucking didn't.

Barry   I've seen the bruises, Steven.

Steven   She stumbled. On the stairs. I went to help / her and –

Barry   Cleo said you would've worked out *some* bullshit story.

Steven   It's the truth.

Barry   She's eight months pregnant, you cunt.

They fight as quietly as possible as –

Steven   *You're* the cunt, not *me*.

Barry   *You're* the cunt.

Steven   *You're* the cunt.

Barry   *You're* the cunt.

Steven   *You're* the cunt.

Barry   *You're* the cunt.

Steven   *You're* the –

Liz *comes back with cup of tea –*

Steven *and* **Barry** *snap apart –*

Liz   One tea three sugars!

Barry   Thanks, Mum. Lovely.

Liz   That enough milk for you?

Barry   It's perfect.

Liz   I can put some more in.

Barry   It's made just right, Mum. As always.

Liz   I was just telling your brother what it's like to live round here.

Barry   I told him you wouldn't like it.

Liz   I don't.

Barry   Mum likes her things around her, I said.

Liz   Oh, I do.

Barry   She likes people to gossip with.

Liz   Oh, I do.

Barry   She'll miss her garden.

Liz   Oh, I do.

Barry   And all the things you had to leave behind, Mum.

Liz   My lovely wardrobe. Solid walnut. The dressing table too.

Steven   They were junk.

Liz   Steven!

Barry   They were *antiques*.

Liz   They were.

Steven   Veneered chip board.

Liz   What's he going on about?

Barry   No idea.

Steven   We had to pay people to take the crap away.

Barry   He's getting a bit wound up I think, Mum. Violent you could say.

Steven   Shut up, Barry.

Liz   Don't talk to your brother like that.

Barry   That's the *real* Steven showing his colours – Has he told you about Debbie?

Liz   What –? Oh. Yes. I don't blame her. Rats. Nasty.

Steven   I told Mum. Debbie thinks we've got rats. She's gone to live with Cleo till it gets sorted out.

Barry   Jesus! You believe that? Mum?

Liz   What, dear?

Barry   The rats?

Liz   Well, all houses can have rats. Even ones that cost a fortune.

Steven   It didn't / cost a fortune.

Barry His place has *not* got rats. Unless it's *him*. Unless *he's* the bloody rat!

Liz Now, now, don't call your brother names.

Barry *Why* not? What would you call someone who hit their wife?

Liz 'Hit their –'? I can't follow you sometimes.

Barry I'll say it slowly then.

Steven He's fucking drunk.

Liz Don't swear.

Barry You *know* I'm not drunk.

Liz We're so proud of you, Barry.

Barry *Mum!* Listen to me! . . . Your eldest son here hit his wife.

Steven Don't listen to him.

Barry In the face.

Steven *What?!* – Jesus! He just makes things up! / He always has!

Barry Punched her. Last night. As a result she, quite rightly, has packed her bags and left him. Now, Mum, what bit of that didn't you follow?

Slight pause.

Liz Drink your tea, dear.

Barry Jesus!

Liz Who wants biscuits?

Steven Yes, please, Mum.

Liz I've got some special ones.

Barry Why do you always bloody believe him? Eh? Every fucking time.

Liz   Oh, the language!

Goes to kitchen.

Barry   Steve says it so it must be true!

Steven   Why don't you just fucking drop it?

Barry and **Steven** *fight as quietly as possible again as –*

Barry   Oh. Yes. That's the way it works in this family. Believe what you wanna believe. Twist this. Ignore the other. That's how we fucking survive.

Liz *returns with –*

Liz   Biscuits!

Barry and **Steven** *have snapped apart –*

Barry   Right, Mum? *Eh?*

Liz   What?

Steven   Don't / listen, Mum!

Barry   You believe him because he wraps all the painful stuff in feathers and flowers. Makes it all safe and cosy. You can't feel the broken glass inside.

Liz   He's making my head spin.

Steven   Mine too.

Barry   Remember when I did that drawing of Dad?

Liz (*at* **Steven**)   What's he going on about?

Steven   No idea – Shut it, Barry!

Barry   I did a drawing of Dad in the canal. At school. I spent ages on it. The teachers encouraged me. Said it was good for me. And it was. Fuck knows, I couldn't talk about it at home. The headmaster put it in the open day exhibition. And what did you do, Mum? When you came to the open day and saw it. What did you do?

Liz   . . . It was a long time ago.

Barry   You tore it down.

Liz   No!

Barry   You tore it down. Tore it into pieces. You shouted at the headmaster. You hit me, Mum. Remember that? Round the face.

Liz   I've never hit either of you boys. *Have* I, Steve?

Steven   Never.

Liz   Not once.

Barry   My nose bled.

Steven   Told you! Makes things up!

Barry   The headmaster said if it wasn't for the pressure you'd been under he would've called the police.

Liz   *What* pressure?

Barry   Dad killing himself!

They all freeze.

Long pause.

Then –

Liz   Biscuits?

Offers biscuit to **Steven**.

Steven   Thanks, Mum.

Liz *takes a biscuit.*

Steven *and* **Liz** *eat biscuits.*

Slight pause.

Barry *dials on his phone.*

Barry   Ask Debbie yourself, Mum.

Steven   Barry.

Barry (*at* **Steven**)   If you've got nothing to hide what's the problem?

Liz   I really don't want to –

Barry (*into phone*)   Deb, Mum wants a word.

Holds phone out.

Beat.

Steven   You don't have to do this, Mum.

Barry   Mum. *Please.*

Beat.

Then –

Liz *takes phone.*

Liz   Hello, love, how are you? . . . Fine, fine . . . Steven tells me you've got rats so you've gone to stay with –

Barry   Don't! Just . . . just ask her what happened.

Liz   I *am* asking.

Barry   You're not!

Snatches phone back.

(*Into phone.*) Tell Mum why you left, Deb. The truth . . . No, no, the *truth*. Okay? . . . Okay.

Gives phone back to **Liz**.

Liz (*into phone*)   Can you hear all this, love? I'm afraid to open my mouth in case I say something wrong at the moment. Anyway, we've got our orders . . . Tell me.

Listens as –

Mmm . . . Yes . . . I see . . . Mmm . . . Mmm . . . No, no, of *course* I understand . . . Don't cry, love, it'll all be fine. You'll see . . . Bye now.

Hangs up.

Gives phone back to **Barry**.

Barry   Well?

Slight pause.

Liz (*at* **Barry**)   How can you tell such lies?

14

Steven*'s house.*

Steven *and* **Liz**.

Steven   Why . . . why didn't you ring?

Liz   I *did* – Oh, you need a bath!

Looks round.

Don't tell me you've been eating takeaways!?

Steven   When . . . *when* did you?

Liz   What?

Steven   Ring.

Liz   All bloody morning.

Steven   'All –'? What's the time?

Liz   Two o'clock.

Steven   Jesus. *Two?*

Liz   I rang the office. Couldn't get anything out of that Janis woman. In the end I phoned Marky-boy.

Steven   What did he say?

Liz   Enough to bring me here.

Picks up dirty clothes.

Don't you know how to work the washing machine yet?

Steven   Eh?

Liz   Washing machine.

Steven   It's in the kitchen.

Liz *goes to kitchen.*

Liz *(from kitchen)*   My God! When did you last do the washing up?

Beat.

Returns with refuse sack.

Steven   How did you get here?

Liz   Bus.

Steven   Oh, Mum.

Liz   I've buried two parents and a husband, I'm more than capable of catching a bus.

Starts picking up rubbish etc.

Steven   Don't.

Liz   It's not gonna clean itself.

Steven   *I'll* do it.

Liz   You're not well.

Steven   I'm fine.

Liz   You've got a fluey bug thing.

Steven   No, no, / I'm fine.

Liz   Steven. You've got a fluey bug thing. Listen to Mum. You've got a fluey bug thing and Mum's here to help. Sit down . . . Sit down, Steven. You've got a fluey bug thing and you need to sit down. You need to do what Mum says and sit down. Now.

Steven *sits.*

Liz   It's no good getting rid of the rats and then letting the house get into a state like this. Debbie'll take one look at it and go straight back to her sister's. And I wouldn't blame her. The baby's due in two weeks, Steven. *Two weeks.*

Steven   I know.

Liz   Well, *look* like you know. I said to Debbie –

Steven   You've spoken to her?

Liz   Of *course* I have. She's my daughter-in-law. I said, 'The rats must've gone by now, love,' I said. 'Rats don't last forever.' She said, 'Yeah, Liz, I think you're right.' I said to her, 'Of course I'm right,' I said. 'Why don't you go back home where you belong?' She said, 'Oh, Liz, it's difficult to talk about.' I said, 'Debbie,' I said, 'I'm family and you can tell me anything.' She said, 'Well, Steve's been acting a bit . . . odd lately, Liz.' I said, 'Odd, love? Can you explain it any more than that?' And she said, 'No, Liz, I can't.' I said, 'Don't you worry about a thing, Debbie, love. I know *exactly* what's wrong with Steven. He's got a touch of the fluey bug thing, that's all. I'll go round and see him.' And here I am – There! That's a bit tidier now. Don't it look better? . . . *Don't* it?

Steven   . . . Yes.

Liz   Course it does.

Takes full refuse sack outside and –

Returns with duster as –

Your dad used to have this fluey bug thing. He used to have it so bad you could almost see the fluey bugs hovering in the air all round him. If you got too close, you could feel yourself catching it too. You could feel it infect your blood. Like being sucked down a plug hole – That's what it felt like. Scared me I don't mind telling you. 'You can stay in your shed,' I told him. And that's what he did. For weeks and weeks sometimes. I made a little bed for him under his desk. Very cosy. I'd leave trays of food outside the shed door for

him. When he was finished he'd put them back outside.
Sometimes he left little notes on the tray telling me he loved
me. He didn't like to be looked at when he got the fluey bug
thing. He covered the shed windows with sheets of
newspaper. Gradually it sort of wore off. Your dad built up
his antibodies – There! Cleaner! You see what Mum does?
You're gonna need some help when the baby's born. Debbie
won't be able to cope. She's not the sort. You know that. I
could live here. In that spare room at the back. That's a
lovely room. Most of my stuff's here in the cellar anyway. We
could all be one big family. Wouldn't that be lovely?

Leaves room.

Returns with glass of water and some tablets.

Hands water to **Steven**.

Liz   Here.

Holds out tablets.

Steven   What're these?

Liz   Aspirin.

Steven   I don't need aspirin.

Liz   Yes, you do.

Steven   I don't.

Liz   You do.

Liz *continues to hold out tablets.*

Beat.

Steven *takes aspirin.*

Liz   When your dad was sure all his fluey bug thing had
gone he'd come out of the shed. I'd make him take all his
clothes off before I let him back into the house. I'd throw the
lot away. Then I'd run him a hot bath and pour some
disinfectant into it. Your dad would soak for ages. I'd shave

him as he lay there. Then I'd cook him a shepherd's pie for dinner – his favourite, remember? – and we'd eat it on trays in front of the telly, just like normal. Just like nothing had ever happened. We never talked about the fluey bug thing once it was over. What was the point? We all get under the weather now and again. Talking – brooding – that don't do any good. You have to get over it. You have to move on. Otherwise you might be sucked down that plug hole and never manage to claw your way back up.

Beat.

Give me the glass.

Slight pause.

Give me the glass.

Slight pause.

Glass!

Steven *gives her the glass.*

Liz *takes glass to kitchen.*

15

Steven I remember . . . burnt bits of paper . . . I found them in the big metal drum. Pages from Dad's notebooks. Burnt edges. Crumbling . . . I take them up to my room. I lay them on my bed . . . Careful . . . Piece them together . . . There's a drawing of a . . . a tree! . . . And words! . . . Words about me . . . me and – I won't say anything bad about you, Dad! Edges crumble to black snow. I won't break my promise! Black snow on my side of the red ziggy-zaggy. Get it clean! Get it clean! Black snow on my fingertips. Get it clean! It'll be our secret. Get it clean! Black snow in my mouth. Lips sealed. Forever, Dad. Lips sealed.

16

The cellar.

Steven *is on floor.*

Barry (*calling, off*)   Steve?

Slight pause.

(*Off*) Steve?

Steven *stirs.*

Barry (*off*)   Steven?

Steven   . . . Barry?

Barry (*off*)   Where are you?

Steven   Here!

Barry (*off*)   Where?

Steven   Cellar!

Barry *appears.*

Barry   What the fuck you doing down here?

Steven   Safer.

Barry   Stinks like a brewery.

Steven   Sorry.

Barry   What's wrong with the light?

Steven   Took the bulb out.

Barry   *Why*, for fuck's sake?

Stumbles on something.

Jesus Christ, I can't see a fucking – Upstairs!

Steven   No!

Barry   Steven. I've just driven all the way from Manchester. Okay? In the fucking rain. In the fucking cold. I am *not* in

the mood for playing games. So listen *very* carefully. Okay?
. . . You listening?

Steven   . . . Yes.

Barry   Debbie's in hospital.

Steven   Hospital?

Barry   She's in labour, for fuck's sake. She and Mum've been trying to get hold of you all day. In the end they rang me.

Steven   Why?

Barry   Fuck knows. Because, I tell you, I don't give a shit. But now I *am* fucking here I'm gonna do what I've been asked to do so – Up! Come on! I'll make you a cup of coffee.

Grabs **Steven**.

Steven   No.

Barry   Steven!

Steven   No! No! *NO!*

Pushes **Barry** *off*.

Barry   Have you gone fucking crazy? *Have* you?

Steven   I can't go back up there! Please don't make me. I need to stay in the dark . . . Please, brov. *Please.*

Slight pause.

Barry *lights cigarette lighter.*

Steven   No light.

Blows out lighter.

Beat.

Barry *lights lighter again.*

Steven *blows it out.*

Barry   Stop it, Steve!

Lights lighter.

Steven   It has to be dark.

Barry   Why?

Steven   I can't see it in the dark.

Barry   See what?

Steven   The ghost.

Blows out lighter.

Barry   Debbie said you might talk like this.

Steven   She *told* you about the ghost!

Barry   There is no fucking ghost!

Lights lighter.

Steven   There is.

Blows out lighter.

Barry   There isn't.

Lights lighter.

Steven   There is.

Blows out lighter.

Barry   There isn't.

Lights lighter.

Beat.

Then –

Steven *hides his face from light.*

Barry *notices candelabrum (with candles).*

Barry   Fuck me! Thought Mum had chucked all Dad's stuff.

Picks up candelabrum.

Steven   Don't light it.

Barry   Why?

Steven   It makes the shadows move.

Barry   What's wrong with that?

Steven   Like being in the shed again.

Takes unlit candelabrum from **Barry**.

Beat.

Barry   Steve . . . I don't know what's going on. You've got yourself into some kind of . . . state over something. My guess? Janis.

Steven   Janis?

Barry   Fucking another woman. Baby on the way. / Major head fuck in anyone's books.

Steven   No, no, no, no.

Barry   That's what Debbie thinks all this is about.

Steven   She's wrong.

Barry   Cleo thinks so too.

Steven   She's always hated me.

Barry   Of course she fucking hasn't.

Steven   You *know* I wouldn't cheat on Debbie, brov. You *know*.

Barry   No. I don't. I don't know fuck all about you. I never have.

Beat.

You know what you're like to me, Steve? The fucking Kennedy assassination. An enigma in a . . . a mystery in a whatsit, or whatever the fucking phrase is. But – hey! – that's what family life is like, eh? Each one of us are either sitting in the back of a car waiting for a bullet. Or sitting at a window in a building waiting to pull the trigger. Or loading a gun waiting to shoot the man who pulled the trigger. The trick is – while all this is going on – to comment on how beautiful Dallas looks in the sunshine. You get me?

Steven   . . . No.

Beat.

Barry   Listen. I promised your wife I'll get you to the hospital. She needs you. In the middle of unimaginable fucking pain – whose name does she call out? Yours! Why? Another fucking mystery in a whatsit. So . . . okay, I'll do my brotherly duty. And then, brov, I will fuck off. Not just back to Manchester. But as far as I fucking go. Australia. California. If I'm lucky enough to get my hands on a fucking spaceship I'll warp speed it to the other side of the fucking universe. *That's* how far I want to go. And once I've fucked off this far I'll never – never! – want to see or hear anything from you ever again. Not you. Not Debbie. Not Mum. I want to forget all about the bloody lot of you. Now get your act together. No bullshit.

Heads upstairs.

Steven   Did Debbie tell you about the T-shirt?

Barry *stops, turns to face* **Steven**.

Barry   . . . *What* T-shirt?

Steven   The ghost. The ghost of the boy I've been was seeing.

Barry   She mentioned the ghost stuff but nothing / about a –

Steven   He was wearing the same T-shirt. Every time I saw him. The shirt had something drawn all over it. It looked like the boy had drawn them himself.

Barry   . . . Drawn what?

Steven   Lots and lots of them.

Barry   Lots of *what*, Steven?

Steven   Each one a different colour!

Barry   What was drawn on the fucking T-shirt?

Beat.

Say it! . . . *Say it!*

Steven   . . . Stars.

Barry *hits* **Steven**.

Steven *falls.*

Beat.

Barry *lights candelabrum.*

Barry *sits close to* **Steven**.

Barry   . . . Dad's funeral – Shall we start there?

Steven *doesn't respond.*

Beat.

Barry   The service was just about to start when . . . when the man . . . turned up and – Can't fucking say it. Fuck! *Fuck!*

Slight pause.

The man – he talked to Mum at the entrance to the chapel. I said to you, 'Who's that, brov?' You said, 'I don't know.'

Beat.

The man sat in the back row. Mum sat between us on the front row. You asked who the man was. Mum said, 'He used to live next door to Dad. Years ago. When your dad was a boy.' I kept looking back at the man. You know what I remember the most? He was the only one crying as much as me. Mum was crying. But tasteful. Like she didn't want to spoil her make up. You didn't cry at all. Not one fucking tear.

Steven *doesn't respond.*

Beat.

Barry   After the funeral . . . this man – he came up and spoke to us. You and me. Mum was talking to her friends from work. The man told us he used to help Dad with his homework. He said Dad was very good at writing. He said. 'I lost touch with your dad when his mum moved away. But I kept some of his poems. Would you like to see them?' I said, 'Yes, please.' The man looked at you and said, 'Why don't you and your brother come round next Friday afternoon.' He told you his address. He didn't write it down. He just kept saying it over and over until you could repeat it back. The man said, 'Best not to tell your mum. Memories of your dad's childhood – they might upset her. We don't want to do that, do we?' We both said we didn't want to do that. And then . . . then the man took you to one side. He put something in your hand and said, 'Treat yourself and your brother.' He'd given you some money. I didn't know how much. Later you bought me . . . what was it, Steve? Remember?

Steven *doesn't respond.*

Barry   One of those join-the-dots books. Join the dots to get a picture. Remember now?

Steven *doesn't respond.*

Barry   . . . All that week you kept saying to me, 'Bet you can't wait to see Dad's poems, eh, brov?' On and on. 'Three days to Dad's poems.' 'Two days to Dad's poems.' 'Tomorrow – Dad's poems.' By the time the day arrived I was – Fuck! I was almost hysterical. Wasn't I? I was practically *begging* you to take me to see the man. Oh, you played it so cool. You had other things to do. Perhaps you wouldn't have *time* to take me. But in the end you took me. We walked the whole way. And we took all the back streets. As if you didn't want anyone to see us. The man lived in this big house on the corner. There was a tree in his front garden. I was so fucking excited. I kept tugging at your hand. You kept telling me to calm down. You rang the door bell. The man opened the door. He was wearing black jeans and a sky-blue shirt. Button up. One of the buttons was missing. We went into his living room. The curtains were pulled and I asked him why. He said, 'I have a very bad headache. They're called migraines.' I said, 'Mum gets those all the time.' The man said, 'Would you like something to drink?' We did. He got us some Cokes. We sat down and talked about Dad. He told us how good at writing Dad was. He said, 'Your dad was destined to be a great poet. It's a shame he died so young. Just thirty-five.' We both giggled at the idea of thirty-five being young.

Beat.

The man said to me, 'Would you like to see your dad's poems now?' And I said, 'Yes.' And the man said, 'Come on, then. They're upstairs.' And the man stood up. And I stood up. But you didn't. I said, 'Come on, Steve. Dad's poems.' The man said, 'I don't think your brother's interested. Is that right, Steven?' And you nodded. I remember being really angry. I felt like hitting you. I said to the man, 'Forget him!' The man held my hand. And I went upstairs with him. Remember?

Steven *shakes his head.*

Beat.

Barry   When I came back down I was crying so much I couldn't catch my breath. The man said to you, 'Your brother found it all a bit too emotional, I think.' The man got us some more Cokes. You were sitting on the sofa. The man said to you, 'I've given your brother one of your dad's poems.' You said, 'He'll like that.' You wouldn't look at me. I wanted you to look at me. But you wouldn't fucking look. I said I wanted to go. You said we couldn't go till I stopped crying. And I knew . . . if I wanted to get home then I had to stop crying somehow. So I thought of other things. I thought of the way Dad swung me up and put me on his shoulders. After a while I managed to stop crying. I dried my face on my T-shirt. When I was totally calm you said, 'Okay. Let's go. Mum will be wondering where we've got to.' We all stood up. The man led us to the door. Then a thought occurred to him and he said, 'Oh, Steven.' And he took you to one side. Just like he did in the cemetery. And he put money in your hand. Only this time I could see how much. And it wasn't just pocket money. It was notes. A *lot* of money. You put the money into your back pocket. The man said to you, 'Perhaps your brother would like to come back next week for another poem.' You said, 'Perhaps he would.'

Steven   . . . No.

Beat.

Barry   On the way home – again we walked, again the back streets – you said I mustn't mention this to Mum. It will upset her. And we didn't want to upset Mum, did we? You said, 'It's our secret. Lips sealed.'

Steven   No, no, / no, no, no.

Barry   When we got home I said, 'Do you want to see Dad's poem the man gave me?' You didn't answer. I took a folded sheet of paper out of my back jeans pocket. I remember it was damp with my sweat. I gave it to you. You sat on the edge of your bed and you opened it. And you studied the piece of paper like you were reading something. Only you weren't reading something, were you, Steve. You weren't reading something because the paper was blank.

Steven   '*B-blank*'? What do / you mean?

Barry   There was nothing on it, Steve. You *know* there wasn't. You bloody *know*!

Beat.

We didn't talk about the man for the rest of the week.

Steven   We . . . we *did*.

Barry   No. Not until next Friday when you said to me, 'I bet you want another one of Dad's poems, don't you.' I said, 'Please don't take me back to the man, brov.'

Steven   You never said *anything* / like that.

Barry   We walked the whole way again.

Steven   The buses were a nightmare! We *agreed* to walk!

Barry   We didn't.

Steven   We did!

Barry   No. And again the back streets.

Steven   It was a short cut!

Barry   It wasn't.

Steven   It *was*.

Barry   I felt sick with fear.

Steven   You were sick with excitement.

Barry   I kept tugging at your hand.

Steven   Excitement! You *see*?

Barry   I wanted to get away.

Steven   You couldn't *wait* to get there.

Barry   No!

Steven   Yes! You were pulling my arm.

Barry   *You* were pulling *me*.

Steven   *You* were pulling *me*.

Barry   You rang the door bell.

Steven   That's right.

Barry   The man opened the door.

Steven   That's right.

Barry   He was wearing jeans and a button-up shirt.

Steven   I can't remember exactly / what he was –

Barry   Black jeans. Sky blue shirt. One of the buttons was missing.

Steven   Alright, alright.

Barry   We went into his living room.

Steven   Yes.

Barry   The curtains were closed again.

Steven   A *little* bit closed.

Barry   The man said to me, 'Would you like to see some more of your dad's poems now?' You said, 'I'm sure he does. Don't you, Barry?'

Steven   What if I did?

Barry   'What if –?' Jesus, Steve! *Jesus!*

Steven   I can see Dad's poems now. His handwriting. / His doodles and scribbles.

Barry   You let the man take me upstairs again! You *let* him! And again I came down crying. And again . . . you took the fucking money.

Steven   I was doing it for *you*.

Barry   For . . . for *me*?!

Steven   It was important you had . . . these memories of Dad all to yourself.

Barry   To *myself*.

Steven   To . . . to help you talk about Dad.

Barry   I never *stopped* talking about Dad.

Steven   You hadn't mentioned him *once*.

Barry   It was you and Mum who never / fucking mentioned him.

Steven   You hadn't cried.

Barry   It's *all* I did!

Steven   It was all . . . inside you. Locked up.

Barry   No.

Steven   Mum was so worried.

Barry   No!

Steven   *I* was worried.

Barry   Why're you doing this?

Steven   Because it's the truth.

Barry   It's not.

Steven   It *is*. Me and Mum didn't know what to do. And then – Yes! This man came to the funeral. He talked to you about Dad. He said he had some poems Dad wrote. You begged me to take you to see them. But . . . oh, I wasn't sure what to do. *Should* I take you or *shouldn't* I take you. I . . . I asked someone for advice! *That's* it. Who *was* it now? . . . One of my school teachers, I think.

Barry   No.

Steven   You're right. It was my *head*teacher.

Barry   No. *No.*

Steven   You can't be *sure*, though, brov. Well, *can* you? After all, I was a child myself. You may *think* of me as being all grown up at that time but I *wasn't*. I needed help. Advice. Guidance, brov! I needed guidance! You can't say I *didn't* ask my headteacher. Can you? . . . *Can* you?

Barry   . . . I . . . I . . .

Steven   Ooo, you're not sounding too confident, brov. Not confident at all. Whereas me? I am *very* confident. Very confident indeed. Listen. I asked my headteacher if it would help you to meet one of Dad's old neighbours and see Dad's poems. Does that sound like a confident voice? I think it does.

Barry   Don't, Steve.

Steven   The headteacher told me it *would* help. They asked me to – No! They *told* me to take you there. You see how it all comes flooding back?

Barry   Stop it.

Steven   I did as I was told. I took you to see this man. The man gave you a poem Dad had written. Oh, it was lovely. Decorated with Dad's doodles. You cried a lot, yes, but . . . oh, you were so much better afterwards.

Barry   You bastard.

Steven   It was like all the grief was leaving you. Everyone noticed the difference. I took you back to see the man for a few weeks after that.

Barry   It was months. *Months!*

Steven   Eventually you got fed up with going. The man understood. He said he was glad to've been of help.

Barry   Steve . . . we've got to talk about this.

Steven   We *are* talking about it, Barry. Don't you see that? And about time too, if you ask me. Long overdue. I'm so grateful you brought it up. Wasn't quite sure how we'd ever do it myself but now we have . . . oh, I feel so much better. Do *you*, brov?

Barry   Please . . .

Steven   The man sent Christmas cards for a few years. Addressed to all of us. We sent cards back. Sometimes we enclosed a little photo we thought he might like. That one of you wearing that T-shirt you drew stars on. Each one a different colour. Remember that? Oh, it was so well done, brov. I wouldn't mind a shirt like that now. You could mass produce them. I'd help set you up. Your own online store. Or perhaps a stall. Camden Market or somewhere. Appeal to you? Why don't we do that? You interested?

Beat.

Perhaps not.

Starts looking for something.

What happened to the man in the end? Do you know, brov?

Beat.

He must be dead by now, don't you think? Perhaps it was nine months ago. Perhaps Mum was invited to the funeral. Perhaps Mum told you about it. Perhaps she told me. Mum didn't want to go. I don't blame her. The man wasn't anything to us. Not really. Not now. It was all so long ago – Eureka!

Finds light bulb.

There was a photo of Cleo in the local newspaper the other day. You see it? Janis pointed it out to me. Just after I fucked her – Only joking!

Screws in light bulb.

The Adventures of Snow White. That's the show Cleo's in. Pantomime. She's Snow White. I would have thought the Wicked Queen was more her type – Only joking. Have you fucked Cleo, brov? Debbie said you did. Or you wanted to. Or Cleo wanted to. You fucked Janis, didn't you? Marky-boy said you did. Or did he say you fucked him. Or wanted to. Fuck me, the possibilities. Endless.

Turns light on.

There! . . . Blow the candles out, brov.

Barry *doesn't move.*

Steven   Blow the candles out.

Barry *doesn't move.*

Steven   Blow the candles out.

. . . **Barry** *starts blowing the candles out.*

Steven   She was in a crystal coffin. Cleo. In the photo. It looks good. The show! We should see it! Shall we do that? All of us. Big family night out. Me, you, Mum, Debbie. That's if the birth goes okay. It could be a stillborn or something. Very common, I hear – Oh! You can put the candelabrum down now, brov.

Barry *doesn't move.*

Steven   You can put the candelabrum down now.

Barry *puts the candelabrum down.*

Steven   Not there.

Beat.

Then –

Barry *moves candelabrum.*

Steven   Not there. Jesus, brov. Don't you know where candelabra go? They go here.

Puts candelabrum in box.

That's the place for candelabra. Can you remember that in future, please – I've just thought. If the baby *is* born alive *and* survives . . . You'll be an uncle. How does that feel? Uncle Barry. I know, I know, bit of a shock. You know what I think you need? . . . A drink.

Gives **Barry** *a bottle.*

17

Steven's *house.*

Steven *and* **Liz**.

Debbie (*singing, over baby alarm intercom*)
   Twinkle, twinkle, little star
   How I wonder what you are. (*etc.*)

Liz   Listen to her.

Steven   She's a natural.

Liz   You're a lucky man.

Steven   I am.

Slight pause.

Liz   The baby alarm works a treat.

Steven   Yes.

Liz   Told you I'd find something else to buy.

Steven   It's perfect.

Slight pause.

Liz   I think the cot you bought is a bit . . . big.

Steven   It is a bit.

Liz   You don't mind me saying.

Steven   You can say what you like, Mum. You know that.

Debbie *enters.*

Debbie   Fast asleep.

Steven   Good.

Liz   I said to Steven, 'The baby alarm works a treat.'

Steven   I said, 'It's perfect.'

Debbie   It is, yes.

Slight pause.

More tea, Liz?

Liz   No, no, I'm fine.

Debbie   Sweetheart?

Steven   I'm fine, sweetheart. Thanks.

Slight pause.

Liz   It's so peaceful here.

Steven   Double-glazing.

Debbie   You need it these days.

Steven   You do.

Slight pause.

Liz   You don't mind me staying in the spare room?

Steven   Of course not, Mum – Sweetheart?

Debbie   Stay as long as you like, Liz.

Liz   Honestly?

Steven *and* **Debbie**   Honestly.

Steven's *phone rings.*

Answers it and –

Steven   Yes? . . . I can't talk about it now . . . Well, tell them I've just got back from my brother's bloody funeral and I'm a little tied up. And oh – you can tell them from me, Graffiti Busters is the best fucking cleaning firm in East London and in this business you get what you pay for. If he wants to pay peanuts, he'll get monkeys . . . Look, I've got to go . . . Thanks, Steph.

Hangs up.

Slight pause.

Liz   Is that the baby?

They listen.

Pause.

Steven   No.

Liz   No.

Debbie   No.

Slight pause.

Liz   Your brother was so looking forward to the baby. Your brother would have taught him all about art. Painting. He was going to be a famous painter. Everything was just taking off for him. Wasn't it, Steve?

Steven   It was, Mum.

Liz   It was. You remember that exhibition he had. When he was a student. That was a lovely night, wasn't it?

Steven   It was.

Liz   And Barry's paintings – oh, they were so beautiful. I wanted one for my living room. You remember that, Steve?

Steven   I do.

Liz   But they all sold.

Steven   You were so upset.

Liz   I was happy for Barry.

Steven   Of course. But sad you didn't get one for your living room.

Liz   I think I cried.

Steven   You did.

Liz   I thought I did.

Slight pause.

Is that the baby?

They listen.

Pause.

Steven   No.

Liz   No.

Debbie   No.

Slight pause.

Liz *starts to cry.*

Steven   Oh, Mum. Don't.

Debbie   I'll get her a drink.

Steven   Thanks, sweetheart – Deb's getting you a drink, Mum.

Debbie   Sherry?

Steven   Perfect.

Debbie *pours sherry.*

Steven   You'll feel better after a sherry, Mum – Won't she, Deb?

Debbie   She will – Here, Liz.

Gives sherry to **Liz**.

Steven   Drink it, Mum.

Liz *sips drink.*

Then –

Liz   I knew he should never have bought that bloody motorbike. I had a bad feeling about it. I said to you. Didn't I, Steve? I said.

Steven   You did, Mum.

Liz   Everything was just falling into place for him. He had a new exhibition coming up. He was going to be a famous painter.

Steven   He was, Mum.

Liz   I've lost both parents, a husband and a son. Haven't I suffered enough? Eh? Haven't I suffered enough?

Steven   Oh, Mum. Please. Don't.

Holds **Liz**.

Liz   You . . . you've always looked after me, Steve. Always. Remember after Dad's accident? Those months?

Steven   Yes, yes.

Liz   That was a . . . a strange time, wasn't it. Hard to remember much about it now.

Steven   I know.

Liz   I went down with a touch of that fluey bug thing, didn't I? Oh, it was awful. All I wanted to do was sleep. I couldn't move. You had to do all the housework. Cooking. And every week . . . you bought me a present. You remember that, Steve?

Steven   . . . Yes.

Liz   A little ornament. Glass – He knew I loved glass, Deb. I remember – oh, my favourite thing! He bought me this glass tree. About . . . this big. I put it in the middle of the dining table. Remember?

Steven   Oh, yes.

Liz   The way it sparkled in the sunlight. And then . . . every week . . . you bought me a beautiful glass leaf to hang on the branches – The twigs were shaped like hooks and you . . . hooked the leaves on. Remember? The leaves – they were so . . . so detailed. And every week . . . for months . . . a leaf . . . until the tree – oh, the tree was this . . . this wonderful shimmering thing. It must've cost you a fortune. How could you afford it? Where did you get all that money? I never found out but . . . I'm glad you *did* because . . . that glass tree . . . it saved me. Truly. Saved me.

Slight pause.

Is that the baby?

Steven   No.

Liz   No.

Debbie   No.

Slight pause.

Baby's cry, off.

Blackout.

Printed in the USA
CPSIA information can be obtained
at www.ICGtesting.com
LVHW020848171024
794056LV00002B/461

9 781350 421820